W9-AHZ-292

Understanding World History

Ancient Egypt

Stuart A. Kallen

Bruno Leone
Series Consultant

ReferencePoint
Press®

San Diego, CA

For more information, contact:
ReferencePoint Press, Inc.
PO Box 27779
San Diego, CA 92198
www. ReferencePointPress.com

LIBRARY OF CONGRESS CATALOGING-IN-PUBLICATION DATA

Kallen, Stuart A., 1955–
  Ancient Egypt / by Stuart A. Kallen.
     p. cm. — (Understanding world history series)
  Includes bibliographical references and index.
  ISBN-13: 978-1-60152-152-1 (hardback)
  ISBN-10: 1-60152-152-9 (hardback)
  1. Egypt—Civilization—To 332 BC 2. Egypt—History—To 332 BC I. Title. II. Series: Understanding world history series.
  DT61.K325 2012
  932.01—dc22
                                                          2010052491

Contents

Foreword 4

Important Events in Ancient Egypt 6

Introduction 8
The Defining Characteristics of Ancient Egypt

Chapter One 11
What Conditions Led to the Rise of Ancient Egypt?

Chapter Two 25
The Pyramid Age

Chapter Three 41
The Middle Kingdom

Chapter Four 55
The New Kingdom

Chapter Five 70
What Is the Legacy of Ancient Egypt?

Source Notes 83

Important People of Ancient Egypt 86

For Further Research 88

Index 90

Picture Credits 95

About the Author 96

Foreword

When the Puritans first emigrated from England to America in 1630, they believed that their journey was blessed by a covenant between themselves and God. By the terms of that covenant they agreed to establish a community in the New World dedicated to what they believed was the true Christian faith. God, in turn, would reward their fidelity by making certain that they and their descendants would always experience his protection and enjoy material prosperity. Moreover, the Lord guaranteed that their land would be seen as a shining beacon—or in their words, a "city upon a hill,"—which the rest of the world would view with admiration and respect. By embracing this notion that God could and would shower his favor and special blessings upon them, the Puritans were adopting the providential philosophy of history—meaning that history is the unfolding of a plan established or guided by a higher intelligence.

The concept of intercession by a divine power is only one of many explanations of the driving forces of world history. Historians and philosophers alike have subscribed to numerous other ideas. For example, the ancient Greeks and Romans argued that history is cyclical. Nations and civilizations, according to these ancients of the Western world, rise and fall in unpredictable cycles; the only certainty is that these cycles will persist throughout an endless future. The German historian Oswald Spengler (1880–1936) echoed the ancients to some degree in his controversial study *The Decline of the West.* Spengler asserted that all civilizations inevitably pass through stages comparable to the life span of a person: childhood, youth, adulthood, old age, and, eventually, death. As the title of his work implies, Western civilization is currently entering its final stage.

Joining those who see purpose and direction in history are thinkers who completely reject the idea of meaning or certainty. Rather, they reason that since there are far too many random and unseen factors at work on the earth, historians would be unwise to endorse historical predictability of any type. Warfare (both nuclear and conventional), plagues, earthquakes, tsunamis, meteor showers, and other catastrophic world-changing events have loomed large throughout history and prehistory. In his essay "A Free Man's Worship," philosopher and mathematician Bertrand Russell (1872–1970) supported this argument, which many refer to as the nihilist or chaos theory of history. According to Russell, history follows no preordained path. Rather, the earth itself and all life on earth resulted from, as Russell describes it, an "accidental collocation of atoms." Based on this premise, he pessimistically concluded that all human achievement will eventually be "buried beneath the debris of a universe in ruins."

Whether history does or does not have an underlying purpose, historians, journalists, and countless others have nonetheless left behind a record of human activity tracing back nearly 6,000 years. From the dawn of the great ancient Near Eastern civilizations of Mesopotamia and Egypt to the modern economic and military behemoths China and the United States, humanity's deeds and misdeeds have been and continue to be monitored and recorded. The distinguished British scholar Arnold Toynbee (1889–1975), in his widely acclaimed 12-volume work entitled *A Study of History,* studied 21 different civilizations that have passed through history's pages. He noted with certainty that others would follow.

In the final analysis, the academic and journalistic worlds mostly regard history as a record and explanation of past events. From a more practical perspective, history represents a sequence of building blocks—cultural, technological, military, and political—ready to be utilized and enhanced or maligned and perverted by the present. What that means is that all societies—whether advanced civilizations or preliterate tribal cultures—leave a legacy for succeeding generations to either embrace or disregard.

Recognizing the richness and fullness of history, the ReferencePoint Press Understanding World History series fosters an evaluation and interpretation of history and its influence on later generations. Each volume in the series approaches its subject chronologically and topically, with specific focus on nations, periods, or pivotal events. Primary and secondary source quotations are included, along with complete source notes and suggestions for further research.

Moreover, the series reflects the truism that the key to understanding the present frequently lies in the past. With that in mind, each series title concludes with a legacy chapter that highlights the bonds between past and present and, more important, demonstrates that world history is a continuum of peoples and ideas, sometimes hidden but there nonetheless, waiting to be discovered by those who choose to look.

Important Events in Ancient Egypt

3100 BC
Upper and Lower Egypt are unified by King Narmer, marking the beginning of the First Dynasty.

2560 BC
King Khufu orders construction of the Great Pyramid at Giza.

| 3100 | 2600 | 2100 | 1800 |

3150 BC
Pharaohs of the Naqada Dynasty solidify their power in Upper Egypt, initiating Dynasty Zero.

1994 BC
Pharaoh Amenemhet I founds the Twelfth Dynasty, the first of the prosperous Middle Kingdom period.

2686 BC
The Third Dynasty is founded, marking the beginning of the Old Kingdom era.

1880 BC
The Egyptians begin placing magical spells called *Coffin Texts* inside tombs to serve the dead.

1785 BC
The first known female pharaoh, Queen Sobekneferu, ascends to the throne.

1570 BC
Ahmose I founds the Eighteenth Dynasty, the beginning of the New Kingdom, a period when ancient Egyptian culture was at the height of its power.

1512 BC
Thutmose I becomes pharaoh, makes Thebes the capital of the New Kingdom, and begins expanding the temple complex at Karnak.

332 BC
The Greek king Alexander the Great conquers Egypt, ending nearly 3000 years of rule by pharaohs.

1064 BC
The Third Intermediate Period begins, a time when Egypt was fractured and ruled by foreign pharaohs from different capitals.

1700   1300   900   500   100

1700 BC
The Hyksos invade Egypt and the central state disintegrates, marking the beginning of the Second Intermediate Period.

664 BC
The Late Period begins, initiating an era when Egypt was dominated by Greek, Roman, and Persian cultural influences.

1279 BC
Ramses II begins his 67-year reign, the last period of great wealth and power for ancient Egypt.

1334 BC
The reign of pharaoh Tutankhamen begins and Amun is restored as the chief Egyptian deity.

1483 BC
The great military leader Thutmose III becomes pharaoh. He goes on to create the largest empire in ancient Egyptian history.

1355 BC
Pharaoh Akhenaten claims the deity Aten is the one and only god and attempts to ban the worship of Amun.

Introduction

The Defining Characteristics of Ancient Egypt

More than 3,300 years after his death, the ancient Egyptian king Tut continues to amaze and mystify. Between 2005 and 2010 a museum exhibition about Tut, called *Tutankhamen and the Golden Age of the Pharaohs*, was seen by over 7 million people worldwide. The traveling exhibit was featured at museums in London, Los Angeles, New York City, and elsewhere and generated more than $100 million in ticket sales.

King Tut ascended to the throne in 1334 BC at age nine and died about 10 years later, possibly from sickle cell disease or malaria. The Tutankhamen exhibit featured breathtaking treasures from his reign, including his golden sandals and the bejeweled containers filled with his mummified internal organs.

Tutankhamen is among the most well-known pharaohs because his treasure-filled tomb remained unopened until 1922. But other pharaohs such as Khufu, builder of the Great Pyramid, and Ramses II, a war hero and conqueror, were more powerful rulers. Their temples and tombs remain among the remarkable symbols of ancient Egyptian civilization, which lasted from about 3500 BC to 600 BC.

Keeping Meticulous Records

Besides creating lasting monuments and artistic treasures, the ancient Egyptians were meticulous record keepers. Using a system of writing called hieroglyphs they described their system of government, military triumphs and defeats, and massive building projects. They carved their complex religious beliefs into stone, into works of art, and across the walls of countless monuments and columns.

The meaning of the hieroglyphs was not understood until the nineteenth century when they were deciphered by French linguist Jean-

The golden funerary mask of King Tut—crafted from solid gold and decorated with lapis lazuli, turquoise, carnelian, quartz, and obsidian—is just one of the many treasures that remind contemporary people of a civilization that flourished thousands of years ago.

François Champollion. After this breakthrough, teams of scholars from Europe, the United States, and elsewhere traveled to Egypt to translate the hieroglyphs and make sense of the ancient civilization. Archeologists unearthed temples, monuments, and papyrus manuscripts that had been buried beneath the desert sands for thousands of years. These writings gave life to ancient Egyptian people, from the royal pharaohs and queens to peasants and slaves.

A Common Past

As scholars deciphered the ancient writings, people came to understand, for the first time, the workings of a culture that influenced civilization for thousands of years. But the ancient Egyptians could not control natural forces and problems created by outsiders. Periodic droughts, famines, and invasions weakened the Egyptian state, leading to its eventual downfall. By the time the Roman emperors ruled the region in the first centuries AD, people remembered little of ancient Egypt's grandeur. Most of the indigenous population believed the pyramids and other monuments were created by a race of giants. Ancient buildings, including the pyramids, were treated with little respect, and finely hewn limestone blocks were stolen for construction projects in nearby Cairo.

Even as the world around the pyramids continued to change, ancient Egyptian culture remained alive among a few intellectuals and scholars. Eventually, this ancient learning came to influence civilizations that followed. From classical Greece to the modern age, ancient Egyptian concepts are still alive in philosophy, religion, art, medicine, astrology, and architecture. This is reflected at the twenty-first-century Tutankhamen exhibit, seen by more people than lived in ancient Egypt during the boy-king's reign. Among the glorious treasures of antiquity, today's digital generation continues to find deep connections to humanity's common past in the age of the pharaohs.

Chapter 1

What Conditions Led to the Rise of Ancient Egypt?

The people of ancient Egypt created a rich, complex culture that lasted for three millennia. Without the life-giving waters of the Nile River, however, ancient Egypt would never have existed. As Greek historian Herodotus wrote about the Nile in the fifth century BC, "Egypt is the gift of the river."[1]

The Nile is the longest river in the world, 4,130 miles (6,648km) from Central Africa to the Nile delta at the Mediterranean Sea. About 750 miles (1,207km) of the Nile flows through Egypt where most of the landscape is incredibly harsh. For about 650 miles (1,046km), the Nile runs through a wide valley where sharp cliffs rise up to 1,500 feet (457m) from the riverbed. The Egyptians called the region Deshret, or "red land," after the color of the rocks and sand. The word desert is derived from this ancient term.

Just north of modern-day Cairo, the cliffs end and the Nile splits into branches that form a large triangular delta, about 100 miles (161km) long and 155 miles (249km) wide at the mouth of the Mediterranean. Before 5000 BC, the delta was uninhabitable. Every year, the Nile flooded the region, leaving the land underwater for about three months. Unlike the sandy Deshret region, the delta was filled with fertile, dark soil, deposited by thousands of years of inundation. The ancient Egyptians called this area Kemet, or "black land."

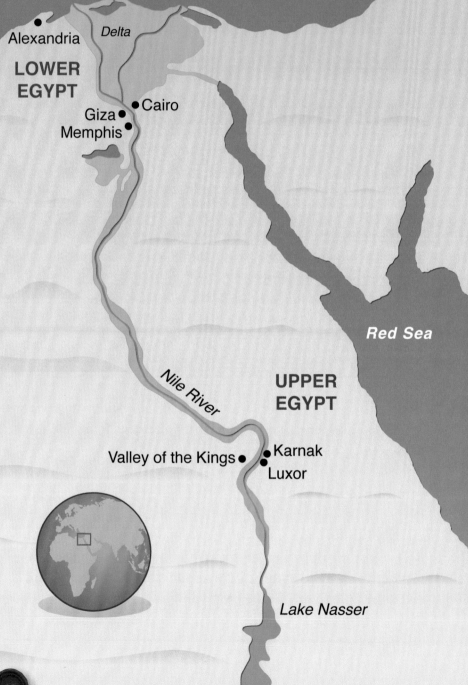

Ancient Egypt

Mediterranean Sea

Alexandria

Delta

LOWER EGYPT

Giza • Cairo

Memphis

Nile River

UPPER EGYPT

Red Sea

Valley of the Kings • • Karnak

Luxor

Lake Nasser

Three Seasons

Around 4000 BC, most ancient Egyptians were wandering hunters. However, small groups began settling down as farmers, cultivating wheat, barley, and other grains and domesticating animals such as cows, sheep, and goats. With an abundant food supply, the population grew.

The climate of ancient Egypt was similar to that of the modern era. The land was a desert with less than 1 inch (2.5cm) of annual rainfall in the north. However, more than 60 inches (152cm) of rain fell on the lands upstream in Ethiopia. This water, laden with rich soil, flooded the Nile delta in early June. The waters crested in mid-August, and the inundation ended in November. This cycle gave the ancient Egyptians their three seasons. The period from late June to mid-October was known as *Aket*, or inundation. From November through February fields were planted and cultivated during the season called *Peret*, or growing. The period between March and May was called *Shemu*, or drought, a time when crops were harvested and processed. Each season was divided into four 30-day months with five festival days. This calendar, which has changed little over the centuries, meant that every year had 365 days.

With Egypt's hot desert climate, farmers could plant and harvest two or three crops a year. Some years were wet and some very dry, causing the height of the river to vary from year to year. A variation of a few inches might mean the difference between prosperity and famine, but good years greatly outnumbered the bad. Century after century the Nile provided the precious gifts of water and fertile soil, allowing a society to develop and grow.

A Common Goal

Ancient Egyptian society was based on agriculture. In order to eliminate drought and starvation, it became necessary to control the Nile. This required the construction of dams and irrigation systems.

The Egyptian irrigation system was the most complex infrastructure of the ancient world. Plots of land were surrounded by canals and dikes made from dirt. During inundation, the Nile rose through a series of canals and was diverted to the fields. When the river fell, the land was fertilized by the exceptionally rich, black silt carried by the waters. Farmers plowed this dirt and planted crops.

The construction and maintenance of the Nile irrigation system benefited all the people of Egypt. The work provided everyone with a common goal and helped bring people together to form a unified state.

The White Land

Because of its geography, Egypt first developed into two kingdoms, Upper Egypt and Lower Egypt. These were ruled by dynasties made up of a succession of hereditary chiefs. Between 3500 BC and 3200 BC, the Naqada Dynasty ruled Upper Egypt, called the White Land.

Upper Egypt was located along the narrow confines of the Nile valley south of modern Cairo. In Upper Egypt the riverbank contained a narrow strip of fertile black soil, bounded by sand and the steep cliffs of the desert plateau. Because the fertile soil was so necessary for agriculture, none was used for building sites. Temples, homes, and other structures were placed on the sand between the fertile strip and the cliffs.

In Upper Egypt various chieftains ruled over about 22 small towns and villages called nomes. Around 3100 BC, the pharaohs, or kings, from the Naqada family were able to solidify their power over the nomes. This allowed the rulers to control the resources of the upper Nile valley. Egyptologists refer to the Naqada Dynasty as Dynasty Zero.

The common people who lived during Dynasty Zero were called the Naqada II culture. Their society was centered in the ancient city of Nekhen, located about 50 miles (80km) south of present-day Luxor. Today Nekhen is known by its Greek name, Hierakonpolis, "City of the Falcon" for the hawk god Horus worshipped by the residents.

Hierakonpolis was one of the first major urban areas along the Nile and its citizens were highly skilled artisans and craftspeople. They created high quality red and black pottery with detailed geometric designs featuring abstract images of people, animals, and boats with many oars. The Naqada II also made jewelry from ivory, lapis, and gold. Production of these goods helped bring wealth to Upper Egypt and increased the powers of the rulers.

In addition to their arts and crafts, another Naqada II cultural development had long-lasting influence on ancient Egypt. The Naqada people created the first hieroglyphic alphabet. The symbols were stylized drawings of plants, animals, buildings, tools, and religious rituals. These early hieroglyphs, later expanded and refined, were the basis for the highly complex system of writing widely used in later centuries.

The Land of the Papyrus Plant

North of Upper Egypt, the marshy Nile River delta, which was lower in elevation, was called Lower Egypt or the Red Lands. Unlike Upper Egypt, where water was a precious resource, Lower Egypt was often too wet. In ancient times the delta was largely untamed wetlands choked

Traditional wooden sailboats known as feluccas sail on the Nile River in southern Egypt beside the red-tinged rocks and sand of the surrounding desert. The development of ancient Egypt owes much to the life-giving waters of the Nile.

thick with reeds. The lowlands also contained the tall marsh plant papyrus later used by the Egyptians to make paper, sandals, baskets, mats, boats, and other goods. The plant was so ubiquitous that residents called Lower Egypt the Land of the Papyrus Plant.

Despite the wet, untamed nature of Lower Egypt, 20 nomes were established in the region between 3500 and 3100 BC. These settlements were built along the banks of the Nile, which split into many branches as the river wound through the marshes to the sea. Living in close proximity to the river, the people of Lower Egypt sustained themselves with an abundance of birds, fish, and other wildlife. Because of the swampy environment of Lower Egypt, less is known about the people who originally settled there. Egyptologist Barbara Mertz explains:

> [We] know more about Upper Egypt than about the Delta. Material that survived in the hot, dry air of Upper Egypt rotted away in the Delta swamps. This fact affects archaeological knowledge in two ways; not only is there less material to be found in Lower Egypt, but also less work has been done there. It is frustrating to excavate in a region where you have to work in water up to your knees, and infuriating to get only indistinguishable lumps of rotted material for your pains. It is no wonder that archaeologists prefer to breathe the . . . desert air of the south, which has preserved even such fragile objects as textiles and painted [artworks].[2]

The town of Merimden beni Salame, about 37 miles (60km) north of Cairo, is one of the few places in Lower Egypt where archeologists have discovered links to the ancient past. Discoveries in the ruins of the village provided clues about Merimden culture.

The Merimden mixed nomadic hunting and gathering with agricultural practices. During inundation, they wandered through the delta region fishing and stalking wild game. They also drove small herds of goats, sheep, and cows to isolated tracts of meadowland and pastures. When the flood waters receded every year, the Merimden settled down to farm wheat and barley.

Flexible Papyrus Paper

The invention of flexible papyrus paper during the First Dynasty allowed Egyptian administrators to keep records and transport information from one region to another. This helped the pharaohs create a large and efficient government. Before paper was invented, scribes carved hieroglyphs into wood or stone palettes, a time-consuming process reserved for only the most important official or historical texts. With the advent of papyrus scrolls, scribes could keep tax records, quickly relay orders to government officials, and create memos and other documents necessary to the centralized bureaucracy.

Papyrus paper also helped advance the social and cultural life of the ancient Egyptians. It provided a format for authors to write poems, stories, and detailed historic accounts for future generations. Reams of papyrus records created thousands of years ago have been invaluable to archaeologists. Since the 1800s, Egyptologists have translated papyri funerary books filled with magic spells and prayers meant to aid the dead on their journey into the afterlife. Ancient school exercises, scientific texts, folk tales, medical prescriptions, and even love poems have also been discovered.

By 3300 BC, a number of villages and town centers stood along the 12 main branches and countless streams in the Nile delta. Because of its proximity to the Mediterranean Sea, Egyptologists speculate that residents of Lower Egypt were involved in a thriving trade with neighboring lands including Greece, Libya, Lebanon, Palestine, Syria, and Jordan. This brought wealth and power to Lower Egypt. It is likely that trade in Lower Egypt also heralded the evolution of an advanced, cosmopolitan culture that attracted skilled workers from many distant regions.

A Common Religion

People in Upper and Lower Egypt spoke the same language and held similar religious beliefs. Ancient Egyptians believed that life continued after death. The dead were buried lying on their sides in the fetal position, as if sleeping or awaiting rebirth. The burial site was treated as a home for the spirit and filled with items, called funerary goods, that were offered as provisions for the afterlife. Archeologists have unearthed graves with traces of grain, fruit, and other foodstuffs, along with bowls and eating utensils. Men were buried with knives, arrowheads, and woodworking tools such as punches, awls, and adzes. Women were entombed with shell and stone beads, fine polished cookware, combs, jewelry, amulets, figurines, and carved plaques.

Religion played an important role in daily life as well as death. With a population dependent on agriculture, the ancient Egyptians focused their worship on the gods of the river, sun, plants, and animals. The god of the Nile, called Hapi, Hep, or Hepi, is the most important deity associated with the river. Although he is a male, Hapi has large, pendulous breasts, which, along with his fat belly, represent the life-giving bounties of the river. Since he provided water, food, and the yearly inundation of the Nile, Hapi was seen as the deity of fertility. And because of his powers over life and death, Hapi was as revered as the sun god called Ra or Re.

Ra was said to have emerged on the first day of Earth's creation and was seen as the father of all beings. Depicted as a pharaoh wearing a sun disk on his head, Ra commanded the chariot of the sun that rode across the sky during the day. Ra lived exclusively in the sky because he was too old to deal with the people and his other creations on Earth. The god Horus had the power to rule Earth in Ra's stead. In this role Horus was the patron of the living pharaohs. He was often depicted as a falcon with its wings spread, perched on the neck of a pharaoh, whispering advice into the ruler's ear. Since the pharaoh was thought to be the earthly embodiment of Horus, each ruler was given a Horus name in addition to other titles. For example, the sixth pharaoh of the Eighteenth Dynasty was known as Thutmose III, and his Horus name was Horus Mighty Bull, Arising in Thebes.

Judging the Dead

The deity Horus was the son of Osiris and Isis. Osiris was said to be an early human king who ruled Egypt, providing his people with civilization and agriculture. Osiris was murdered by his brother Set who chopped up his body and scattered the remains throughout Egypt. Osiris's wife, Isis, is also his sister. Isis picked up the pieces of Osiris and used her supernatural powers to reassemble her brother-husband. The resurrected Osiris became the king of the underworld where his job was to judge the virtue or immorality of each dead person.

Details about the afterlife were recorded in the *Book of the Dead*, a collection of religious and poetic incantations first compiled around 3500 BC. The writings were carved into coffins and the walls of tombs. In later centuries the *Book of the Dead* was printed on papyrus scrolls that were buried with the deceased to help guide them in the afterlife. According to the *Book of the Dead*, Osiris and 42 judges weighed the

Osiris, the Egyptian god of the underworld, sails in his boat (top) and farmers plow their fields (bottom) in this panel from the Book of the Dead. *The spells and rituals for eternal life can be found within this ancient Egyptian text.*

dead person's heart on a scale and balanced it against a feather to see if it was heavy with sin.

The ancient Egyptian pantheon includes hundreds of other major deities. In addition, each nome had its own gods, mostly in the form of animals such as dogs, birds, jackals, snakes, sheep, or bulls. The deities were thought to have magical powers, and amulets of animal gods were buried with the dead. Animal-based deities from the early period eventually transformed into animal-human gods. These were depicted in artwork where animal bodies were attached to human heads, or visa versa.

Uniting the Two Lands

Despite their shared beliefs, residents referred to Upper Egypt and Lower Egypt as the Two Lands because of the evident divisions between the regions. Because of its seaports and trade, Lower Egypt was more cosmopolitan. The wet conditions found there allowed Lower Egyptians to live well, with vineyards and gardens around their homes. Upper Egypt had a more rural character and a large population packed into a narrow strip of fertile land between towering cliffs and harsh desert.

The princes of Upper Egypt were aggressive and organized and saw the rich fertile delta of Lower Egypt as a tempting target for conquest. Egyptologist Cyril Aldred explains, "It was the ambition of the Southern princes [in Upper Egypt] that led them to extend their sway over ever larger tracts of the valley until they had created a unity out of former anarchy, one kingdom out of a conglomeration of rival districts."[3]

Around 3150 BC one of those Upper Egyptian princes, King Narmer (later called Menes or Meni, "the founder") was able to unite the Two Lands through political will or military conquest. In doing so Narmer became ancient Egypt's first pharaoh, initiating the First Dynasty.

Based on a discovery by two English archaeologists in 1897, Egyptologists determined that Narmer united Upper and Lower Egypt. James Quibell and Frederick Green were digging at the site of Hierakonpolis when they discovered an ancient temple containing a fascinating object: a piece of carved slate they named the Narmer palette.

The Narmer palette had pictures on both sides. They were carved to announce the unification of Lower and Upper Egypt under one pharaoh. One side showed a man wearing the red crown worn by rulers of Lower Egypt. He gazes at a row of dead soldiers on a battlefield. Hieroglyphs of a catfish and a chisel spell out the pharaoh's name, Narmer. On the other side of the palette, Narmer wears the white crown of Upper Egypt. He is shown raising a club-like mace with one hand, ready to bring it down on the head of the enemy he clutches with the other hand. A caption above the picture reads, "Pharaoh, the incarnation of the hawk-god Horus, with his strong right arm leads captive the Marsh-dwellers."[4]

Age of the Pharaohs

Ancient Egyptians regarded the unification of Upper and Lower Egypt as the most important event in history, comparable to the creation of the universe. As the uniting force, Narmer was considered a god-king—both a king and a deity.

With the unification of the Two Lands under Narmer, the age of the pharaohs began, marking a period in which pharaohs would rule over Egypt for three millennia. Egypt's population was estimated to number about 200,000 at the time of unification. The population would grow to about 5 million by 2000 BC. With a single god-king controlling all of Egypt, warfare largely ceased and the vast energies of society were channeled into building, learning, and producing food and goods. Through these means, the Egyptians laid the foundations for a culture that would thrive for thousands of years.

During the First Dynasty, power was centralized in a highly organized theocracy, that is, a government based on religion. The god-king, or pharaoh, sat atop this bureaucratic structure and all of the country's economic, political, and religious institutions fell under his royal authority. The government employed soldiers, scholars, servants, bureaucrats, and artisans whose goods and services were used to benefit the upper classes and nobility. These workers developed sophisticated intellectual, artistic, military, scientific, and administrative traditions that served Egyptian civilization for centuries.

United Egypt's Capital at Memphis

Narmer's son Hor-Aha (or simply Aha) became the second pharaoh of the First Dynasty around 3100 BC. One of Aha's first acts was to order the construction of Memphis, a city that would serve as the capital of united Egypt. Memphis was located at the mouth of the Nile delta where it spreads out into a broad triangle. This area was considered the point of balance between Upper and Lower Egypt.

Memphis was home to the royal palace and the central government ministries including treasury, judiciary, and military. Highly placed officials built huge estates surrounded by parks and lakes. The city was also the center of foreign trade, the arts, and most other important aspects of society.

Although little is left of Memphis in modern times, Egyptologists say this seat of government was run in an exceedingly efficient manner—thanks in large part to paper made from papyrus. This flexible paper allowed the government to keep accurate records that aided in the expansion of its powers.

The Respected Scribe

The development of papyrus led to the invention of the reed pen and inks made from black and red pigments. With these new writing tools, the complex hieroglyphs were slowly transformed into flowing cursive script, a simpler and less tedious form of writing. The development of papyrus paper, pen and ink, and cursive writing also led to the growth of a new professional class: scribes who were hired as official record keepers.

Only very educated men could work as scribes and the position was one of the most respected in ancient Egyptian society. As high-ranking record keepers, scribes knew the secrets of the pharaohs and the in-

A Home for the Dead God-King

One of the central beliefs that led to the rise of the powerful ancient Egyptian nation was the notion of an all-powerful pharaoh who was both a human king and a living god who remained alive even after death. This concept led to the design and construction of tombs to house the deceased pharaoh in the afterlife. It also led to the invention of funerary practices that were adopted by the general public in later centuries.

The pharaohs of early dynasties built burial chambers called mastaba tombs, flat-roofed, rectangular structures made from mud-bricks or stone. Bodies were entombed in underground chambers deep beneath the mastaba. These were equipped with goods and supplies for the pharaoh's eternal comfort.

Food was considered of the utmost importance in the afterlife. The pharaoh's relatives ensured fresh food was delivered daily. In case deliveries were interrupted, a tall stone slab was left in the mastaba with a menu carved into it. The Egyptians believed that the written word itself was so magical that by simply writing down the words for foods, they would provide sustenance for the dead god-king.

ner workings of the government. With their pens and papyrus scrolls, scribes supervised bureaucrats and controlled trades and professions.

Scribes also supervised tax collection for the pharaoh. This was an important task in a land where people were heavily taxed to pay for beautiful government buildings and the elaborate centralized bureaucracy in Memphis. Since ancient Egyptians used a barter system instead of money, taxes were collected in products or services. Artisans and craftspeople paid their taxes with jewelry, paintings, sculptures, baskets, furniture, pottery, and so on.

Farmers paid their taxes with grain, livestock, fruit, and other foods. Some of the foodstuffs were preserved and stored by the government for times of famine. In order to assess grain taxes, the height of the Nile inundation was precisely measured with an instrument called a nilometer. If the Nile failed to reach the optimum level, taxes were reduced for the year. Taxes on livestock were based on the size of individual herds, and animals were counted by tax officials every other year. Census takers also counted the number of people in each household, leveling a tax on each servant, slave, and family member.

A Strong Foundation

Around 2950 BC, Hor-Aha's three successors, Djer, Djet, and Den, oversaw further consolidation of the Two Lands into a single state. Artwork began to appear with pharaohs wearing the double crown, a fusion of the red and white crowns of Lower and Upper Egypt. With the powerful natural force of the Nile and a unified Egypt operating under a single powerful pharaoh, the foundation for three thousand years of society and culture was firmly in place.

Chapter 2

The Pyramid Age

Each year more than 8 million people visit the three pyramids in Giza, near present-day Cairo. The largest structure, the Great Pyramid of King Khufu, was built around 2560 BC. It was constructed during an era known as the Old Kingdom, a 500-year period—between 2686 and 2184 BC—considered to be one of the richest and most innovative in ancient Egyptian history. During this era, which encompassed the Third through Sixth Dynasties, approximately 180 pyramids were constructed. For this reason historians often refer to the Old Kingdom as the pyramid age.

During the Old Kingdom the work of the pyramid builders was made possible by developments in Egyptian society. Earlier construction of massive irrigation systems revolutionized agricultural production and provided a steady supply of food to average Egyptians. The well-fed people generated a population explosion that increased the number of workers available for large building projects. The growing population also meant more artisans and designers to create a surplus of art, jewelry, clothing, furniture, and other goods. A portion of this artistic wealth was paid to the pharaoh in taxes and also helped fuel the expansion of trade with other nations. Taxes and trade brought untold riches to the pharaohs who used their wealth to create pyramids.

The Immortal Pharaoh

The ancient Egyptians viewed the pharaoh as an immortal god-king responsible for life, fertility, and the prosperity of the nation. The pyramid was a tomb built to house the pharaoh's mummified remains after death and to hold his vital life force called a *ka*.

The ancient Egyptians believed that each person's ka extended back through previous generations all the way to the gods. The pharaoh,

The pyramids of Giza rise above the desert floor, a testament to the architectural artistry and precision of ancient Egypt's pyramid builders. Their work was most prolific during the 500 years known as the pyramid age.

because of his status as a god-king, was seen as the ka, or life force, of all people. When a pharaoh was entombed, elaborate rituals where held inside pyramids to ensure the survival of the ka, which was said to temporarily leave the body while the corpse was prepared and transformed into a mummy. Egyptians believed that after the pharaoh's body was properly mummified, the ka would return to it.

Mummification

In later centuries, the religious rituals and beliefs concerning the pharaoh were extended to include all Egyptians. During the Old Kingdom, however, only pharaohs, their families, and high-ranking nobles were mummified and utmost attention was paid to their spirits after death.

Each part of the mummification process required complex religious rituals and the entire procedure took around 70 days. The first step in mummification was to remove the brain, lungs, and lower organs—all believed by the Egyptians to be worthless. Next the body was packed in a salt called natron, which dried the tissues and kept them from breaking down. Other internal organs were then removed, some being preserved in pottery or stone vases called canopic jars. At this point, embalming fluids and pastes were applied to preserve the skin and body interior. Finally the body was wrapped in many layers of linen strips with jewel-encrusted magical charms sandwiched between the layers of cloth.

After the mummification process, the pharaoh was transported to his tomb where his ka was reanimated and reunited with his body in an elaborate ceremony. At this time a second type of life force, called the *ba,* assumed greater importance. Unlike the ka, which remained alive through generations, the ba was unique to each individual. When a person died, the ba lived on and continued to eat, drink, travel, and make love. The Egyptians believed that the pharaoh could not utilize the ba if his body decomposed, which made mummification an important necessity.

During the Fifth Dynasty, magical incantations from a script called the *Pyramid Texts* were carved into the pyramids at Saqqara, northwest of Memphis. These texts, which likely existed on papyrus scrolls during the Third Dynasty, were written to guide the pharaoh's ba immediately after death:

> Oho! Rise up . . .
> Take your head, collect your bones,
> Gather your limbs, shake the earth from your flesh!
> Take your bread that rots not, your beer that sours not,
> Stand at the gates that bar the common people!
> The gatekeeper comes out to you, he grasps your hand,
> Takes you into heaven, to you father Geb.
> He rejoices at your coming, gives you his hands,
> Kisses you, caresses you,
> Sets you before the spirits, the imperishable stars. . . .
> Rise up . . . you shall not die![5]

The Pharaoh's Stairway to Heaven

Once the pharaoh's mummy was entombed inside the pyramid, the ba became as important as the body was during life. The *Pyramid Texts* speak of various gifts and jewelry being given to the ba, along with a royal garment made from a leopard pelt. And this was only the beginning of the pharaoh's ba in the afterlife. It was believed the pharaoh ascended to the heavens and spent eternity sailing across the sky in a

The bodies of the dead were preserved for their journey to the afterlife through the process of mummification. Pictured here is a mummy, wrapped in layers of linen strips. Sometimes jeweled charms were placed between the layers of linen.

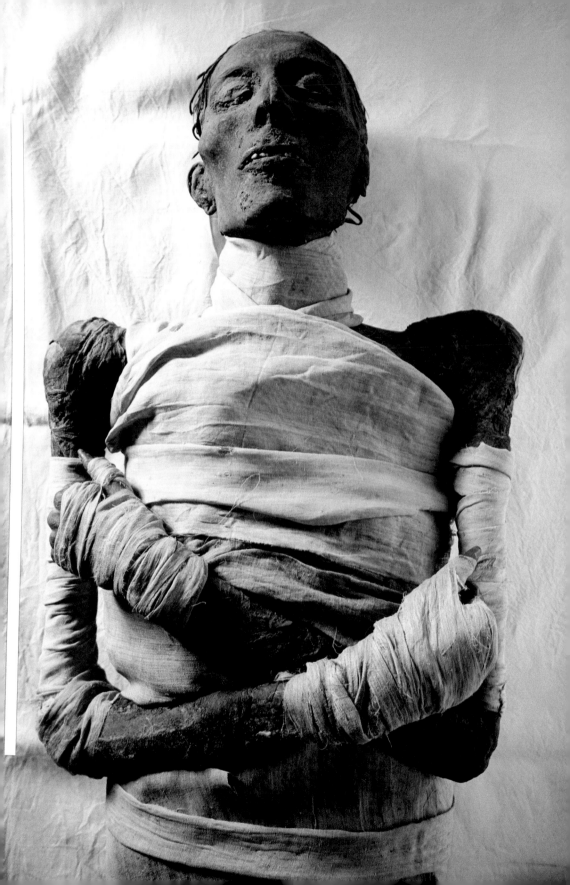

small sacred boat called a bark. Every day the pharaoh would ride in his bark with Ra the sun god, tracking the sun across the sky from east to west.

Egyptologists speculate that the pyramids were built to act as stairways to heaven. When a pharaoh died, his ba climbed up the pyramid to ascend into the sky. While this theory remains unproven, it is known that the massive, complex task of building huge pyramids developed in a very short time. The simple mastaba tombs, built of mud brick during the Second Dynasty grew into incredible stone pyramids within a few decades. Historians trace this remarkable advance in architecture to a single man, Imhotep. He designed the Step Pyramid at Saqqara for King Djoser, the second king of the Third Dynasty whose reign began around 2668 BC.

The Step Pyramid

The Step Pyramid consists of six large mastaba-shaped structures of diminishing size stacked one on top of the other. The pyramid measures about 358 by 411 feet (109 by 125m) at its base and rises to a height of nearly 203 feet (62m). The Step Pyramid is the first building ever constructed with stone masonry, stones that were cut, carved, and stacked by mathematical design rather than rough rocks piled one upon the other.

According to information carved into a statue within the Step Pyramid complex, Imhotep was "The Chancellor of the King of Upper and Lower Egypt, Administrator of the Great Palace, Hereditary Lord, Greatest of Seers, Imhotep, the Builder, the Sculptor, the Maker of Stone Vases. . . . Chief of that Which Heaven Brings, Earth Creates and the Nile Brings."[6] In addition to these powerful positions, Imhotep was the construction foreman for the Step Pyramid.

The construction of the Step Pyramid may have lasted more than 34 years. During this time workers quarried huge blocks of limestone from a nearby cliff with tools made from stone, copper, and wood. The rough-cut blocks had to then be moved across the shallow waters of the Nile to Saqqara. In order to complete this process, the builders had to overcome a major problem. Even during inundation, the Nile waters were not deep enough to float huge limestone blocks or granite beams

A Healthy Diet for a Growing Population

Based on food and drink residues found at excavation sites, archeologists determined that ancient Egyptian peasants had a healthy diet. They subsisted on cucumbers, beans, lentils, peas, and lettuce as well as fruits such as dates, pomegranates, and watermelon. Wealthier citizens consumed a variety of eggs, fish, fowl, beef, and pork, along with wine, carefully labeled as to year and vintage. Egyptian cooks spiced up their dishes with cumin, coriander, parsley, and fenugreek. Cakes and pastries were baked with chocolate-like carob, fruit, and honey.

Beer and bread made from wheat and barley were standard fare for even the poorest Egyptians. Beer was a very popular drink, consumed by children and adults. Women in every home brewed beer, and there were several large commercial breweries along the banks of the Nile. Pharaohs even received beer as payment for taxes. One record shows that the royal court received 130 jars of beer every day. Upon death, nearly every Egyptian citizen was buried with a few jars of beer for consumption in the afterlife.

to the pyramid construction site. Some researchers speculate that the builders dredged deep channels in the Nile to float the stones on raft-like boats but there is no proof that such waterways ever existed. However the massive stones were ferried to the Step Pyramid, they were finally dragged to the building site by teams of men using papyrus ropes. There the blocks were carved into finished stone and somehow lifted into place.

Djoser's Step Pyramid is the oldest surviving stone structure in the world. However, it was buried under drifting desert sands for untold centuries. It was not uncovered until 1926, when French Egyptologist Jean-Philippe Lauer unearthed it from beneath the desert floor. Completing his work in 1994 at the age of 92, Lauer spent 68 years excavating the site, about twice as long as it actually took to build.

A Pyramid Building Boom

While Djoser's tomb was an artistic and engineering feat, its magnificence was soon overshadowed. Around 2613 BC, King Sneferu founded the Fourth Dynasty and embarked on a pyramid building boom that resulted in at least six great edifices. Sneferu's first contribution was a seven-step pyramid at Meidum, about 60 miles (96km) south of modern Cairo.

Sneferu built his pyramid to resemble Djoser's Step Pyramid, but he later ordered another step to be added, bringing the total number to eight. For reasons unknown, about 15 years later Sneferu commissioned his workmen to return to Meidum to remake the step pyramid into a true pyramid by filling in the steps with stones and covering them with a fine white limestone casing. Although the motives remain unclear, it is believed that during that time, new building techniques and architectural advances were discovered that allowed construction with huge slabs of stone rather than smaller blocks.

During initial construction of the Meidum pyramid, Sneferu moved his royal headquarters to Dahshur, where he ordered construction of two more monumental pyramids. The first of these structures was called the "Gleaming Pyramid of the South" by the ancient Egyptians. It is known today as the Bent Pyramid because its sides slope at about a 52-degree angle at the bottom and change to a 43-degree angle about two-thirds of the way to the top. The Bent Pyramid was covered with fine polished limestone. Unlike the other pyramids, which over the centuries were stripped of their stone by locals needing building material, the Bent Pyramid retains this stone.

The Great Pyramids at Giza

Sneferu built several more pyramids and an array of fortresses, palaces, and temples. These buildings were constructed by peasants, a class of impoverished workers who made up about 80 percent of ancient Egypt's population. Peasants spent most of the year farming, while providing a large percentage of their crops as taxes or offerings to the gods and pharaohs at temples. During the three months or so when inundation made farming impossible, peasants were conscripted to work on construction projects or act as laborers for the military. These recruits were placed on labor gangs with criminals and those who had failed to pay their taxes. Conscripts might work in gold mines, excavate stones for construction, or labor on building projects large and small. They were not paid but received food and drink including beer, bread, onions, garlic, and radishes.

Around 2560 BC thousands of workers were conscripted by Sneferu's son Khufu, who ordered construction of the Great Pyramid at Giza. In 443 BC the Greek historian Herodotus visited Egypt and wrote about the construction of the Great Pyramid:

> To some was assigned the [task of] dragging of great stones from the stone quarries in the Arabian mountains as far as the Nile; to others [Khufu] gave orders, when these stones had been taken across the river in boats, to drag them, again, as far as the Libyan hills. The people worked . . . for ten years of time in building the road along which they dragged the stones—in my opinion a work as great as the pyramid itself. For the length of the road is more than half a mile, and its breadth is sixty feet, and its height, at its highest, is forty-eight feet. It is made of polished stone, and there are figures carved on it.[7]

Mountain of Stone

The Great Pyramid of King Khufu, which is one of the wonders of the ancient world. Khufu's pyramid rises 481 feet (146.6m) above the desert floor, and each side of its square base is 756 feet (230.4m) in length. Until 1887, when the Eiffel Tower was constructed in Paris, the Great Pyramid was the tallest structure on earth—a record it held for 440 centuries.

Herodotus estimated 100,000 workers were required to construct this mountain of stone. Modern archeologists put the number of workers at 20,000 to 30,000. Whatever the exact size of the labor force, it undoubtedly took a large number of people to move the 2 million stone blocks that make up Khufu's tomb. The average stone weighed around 2.5 tons (2.27 metric tons), and the largest blocks were up to 70 tons (63.5 metric tons). And some of these rocks were dragged from quarries 500 miles (804km) away. To this day no one understands how these huge rocks were moved to the pyramid or accurately lifted into place without modern equipment such as steel cables, pulleys, power equipment, trucks, and cranes.

Inside the Pyramid

The Great Pyramid was surrounded by a limestone wall over 26 feet (8m) high, which enclosed a courtyard filled with finely carved columns, statues, temples, and sanctuaries. The main part of the Giza complex once held two buildings called mortuary temples. These were built in front of the pyramid not only to honor Khufu's reign but as places where the pharaoh's family and followers could honor his ba and leave offerings. A second mortuary temple was built for two of Khufu's wives.

Khufu's mortuary temple was connected to a funerary building by a long covered walkway over 130 feet (40m) high. Researchers believe that the pharaoh was mummified in the funerary building and transported down the causeway in a full-size boat to the mortuary temple. This passage symbolized the king's passing from the physical world to the underworld.

Inside the pyramid, various interior structures were built to accommodate the mummified Khufu and his ba. The entrance into the pyramid is almost 56 feet (17m) above the ground. This opens into a narrow sloping corridor, known as the Descending Passage, a corridor 3 feet 2 inches (0.96m) high and 3 feet 5 inches (1.04m) wide. It slopes down through the pyramid's building blocks at a steep 26-degree angle for 92.5 feet (28m) and continues through the bedrock under the pyramid for another 99 feet (30m). Like the outer construction of the pyramid, this passage was built with incredible precision—deviating less than 3/8 of an inch from a straight line over the course of nearly 200 feet (61m), half of it through solid rock. In addition, it runs at an exact north-south direction.

The Descending Passage ends at an empty, roughly hewn pit, known now as the Subterranean Chamber. This room is about 46 feet

The high-roofed, limestone hallway known as the Grand Gallery (pictured) sweeps toward the king's chambers inside the Great Pyramid. Although the Grand Gallery looks something like a massive staircase, it has no steps.

(14m) long, 23 feet (7m) wide, and 17 feet (5m) high. It appears to have been left unfinished for reasons unknown. The chamber has some mysterious features, such as a tunnel, wide enough to hold only a single person, that leads from the Subterranean Chamber to a dead end. Why builders struggled to chip this tunnel to nowhere out of solid rock remains a mystery.

Another tunnel, called the Ascending Passage, leads from a hole in the roof of the Descending Passage. The Ascending Passage moves upward into the heart of the Great Pyramid to a room called the Queen's Chamber, although archaeologists have determined that the queen was never meant to be buried there. As it nears the Queen's Chamber, the Ascending Passage turns into a high-roofed hallway now known as the Grand Gallery. It is described by pyramid researchers Robert Bauval and Adrian Gilbert:

> [The] Grand Gallery . . . is in many ways, the most elaborate and mysterious feature of a whole internal system of the Great Pyramid, and words can scarcely do it justice. It runs upward at the same angle as the ascending corridor but instead of being a narrow, crouched tunnel it is [26 feet] high. When you are inside, it gives the impression of being even higher as it sweeps towards the King's Chambers at the top end. It is a very curious structure indeed, for though it looks rather like a massive staircase, there are no steps as such. Yet it appears highly functional and was carefully finished in smoothed Tura limestone . . . as with so much Egyptian architecture, it looks so ancient that it seems almost modern. There is a quasi-inhuman quality about the Grand Gallery that is hard to explain, as though it were not intended for people to walk up and down but to serve some other specialized or specific function.[8]

The King's Chamber

The King's Chamber lies at the top of the Grand Gallery. This room is made from red granite and its workmanship is amazing. It measures 34

Great Pyramid, Amazing Construction

The remarkable features of the Great Pyramid have inspired awe and wonder for centuries. Even in the modern era, researchers have yet to determine how Khufu's tomb was constructed. The pyramid contains enough rock to pave a road 8 feet (2.4m) wide and 4 inches (10cm) deep from San Francisco to New York City. On the face of the pyramid, the flat surface stones were cut within 1/100 of an inch (.25mm) of a perfectly straight line, and all cuts are at perfect 90-degree right angles. The stones were piled upon one another with a gap of 0.02 of an inch (.5mm), thinner than a knife blade, left between them. Even in the twenty-first century, modern builders cannot achieve this sort of accuracy with such heavy stones. The tiny gap between the stones was filled with a white glue-like cement that connected the stones and prevented water from seeping into the cracks. This amazing substance has remained intact for nearly 45 centuries and has a surface hardness stronger than the limestone blocks that it joins together.

In addition to this glue, the cornerstones of the Great Pyramid have balls and sockets built into them, like a modern bridge. This allows the structure to expand and contract with heat and cold, as well as withstand earthquakes. Without this feature, the pyramid would not have remained standing.

feet by 17 feet (10m by 5m), and the chamber's ceiling is 19 feet (5.7m) high, finished with solid granite stones that weigh up to 30 tons (27.2 metric tons) each. They are perfectly smooth and so tightly joined— like the pyramid's facing stones—that the blade of a knife would not fit between the cracks. At one end of the King's Chamber lies a large sarcophagus known as the Granite Coffer, which was obviously in place before the pyramid was finished because it is too large to have been moved through the structure's narrow passageways. The coffer is an engineering miracle in itself, hollowed out from a single block of solid red granite. No one has been able to devise a satisfactory theory on how the Egyptians cut this incredibly hard stone with primitive tools. In any case, there is little evidence that this finely constructed coffer ever held Khufu's mummified body. As Bauval and Gilbert write:

> Although it is believed that this was the final resting-place of Khufu, there is not the slightest evidence of a corpse having been in that chamber, not a sign of embalming material or fragment of any [artifact]. No clue, however minuscule, has ever been found in this chamber or anywhere else in the Great Pyramid. This has led many to suppose that we have not yet found the burial chamber of Khufu.[9]

Without his mummified remains, the only known image of the builder of the world's largest pyramid is a tiny statue—only 3 inches (7.6cm) tall—of Khufu sitting on his throne.

End of an Era

After Khufu's death, around 2566 BC, finishing work continued on the Great Pyramid while Khufu's son, pharaoh Khafre, began work on a slightly smaller pyramid. Khafre also built a monument to guard and protect the pyramids. The Great Sphinx is a colossal statue 240 feet (73m) long and 66 feet (20m) high at its head and was carved from the ragged outcrops left behind at a quarry site where pyramid rocks were mined. The statue has the body of a reclining lion and the face of pharaoh Khafre, complete with his royal headdress and traditional false beard.

The third pyramid at the Giza complex was built by Khafre's son, Menkaure. With about 10 percent of the mass of Khufu's Great Pyramid, Menkaure's tomb is 335 feet by 343 feet (102m by 104m) and rises to a height of around 213 feet (65m).

Inside the Great Pyramid

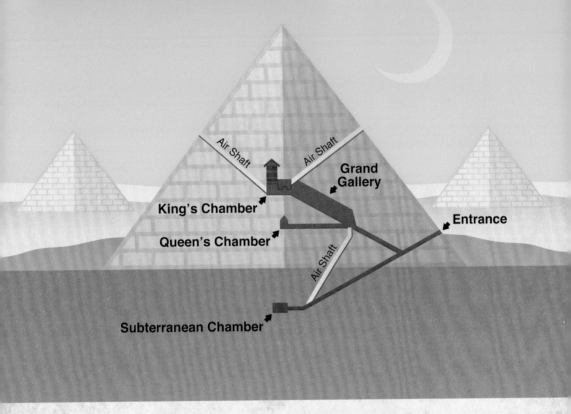

King's Chamber

Queen's Chamber

Air Shaft

Air Shaft

Grand Gallery

Entrance

Air Shaft

Subterranean Chamber

It appears as if work was halted on Menkaure's pyramid before it was completed, and pyramids the size of Khufu's were never attempted again. As the glorious pyramid age of the Fourth Dynasty drew to a close around 2494 BC, several smaller pyramids were constructed. By the Fifth Dynasty, however, construction skills had sharply declined, and the newer pyramids eventually collapsed. Today some of these piles of rubble are barely recognizable as pyramids. Four small pyramids were built by the Sixth Dynasty pharaohs at Saqqara between 2345 and 2181 BC. All of these structures were about 173 feet (53m) high.

Egyptologists are unsure why the architects and engineers of the Fifth and Sixth Dynasties were unable to draw on the experience of the previous pyramid builders. But the quality of the workmanship declined so rapidly that it was as if every skilled Egyptian stone mason and construction worker simply disappeared. Taken as a total, all the pyramids built after the Fourth Dynasty used less than half the limestone used in Khufu's pyramid alone. Some speculate that famine, political upheaval, or a deadly epidemic helped bring about the end of the pyramid age, but historians do not know for sure.

War, Famine, and Anarchy

After the Sixth Dynasty came to a close, around 2170 BC, the central government of the Old Kingdom in Memphis collapsed. Egypt entered into a dark age known as the First Intermediate Period, marked by famine, small-scale civil wars, and social anarchy. As the scribe Ipuwer saw it, "I show you the son as a foe, the brother as an enemy, and a man killing his own father. The wild beasts of the desert will drink at the rivers of Egypt and be at their ease. Men will seize the weapons of warfare, and the land will live in chaos."[10]

Egypt entered into a period of chaos that lasted until 1994 BC, when the Twelfth Dynasty began. Although the Old Kingdom crumbled, it produced an enduring legacy in the Great Pyramids and countless other tombs and temples filled with mummies, artwork, and sacred texts.

Chapter 3

The Middle Kingdom

Historians believe a massive volcanic eruption in New Guinea, an island near Australia, lofted dust and debris high into the atmosphere around 2020 BC. Ancient Egyptians of the Eleventh Dynasty did not know of New Guinea's existence, but the eruption irrevocably altered their lives. The volcanic debris dimmed the sun over Egypt and brought at least four years of cold, drought, crop failures, and famine.

A weak central government provided no help to its people. According to some reports from the time, desperate Egyptians may have resorted to cannibalism. A peasant farmer from Thebes, a city along the Nile River in the area of modern-day Luxor, describes the horrors in a letter to his family: "See! The whole land is perished. . . . See! They are beginning to eat men here! . . . The whole of Upper Egypt died from famine . . . all men ate their children."[11]

Around 2000 BC, the job of saving Egypt fell to the individual nomes and the governors or monarchs who ruled them. They organized agricultural practices and water distribution to benefit the people under their control. The achievements of one of these men, the monarch of the Oryx nome named Amenemhet (sometimes spelled Amenemhat), were later carved into his tomb:

> When the years of hunger happened, I then cultivated all the fields of the Oryx nome as far as the southern and the northern boundaries, giving life to its inhabitants and providing its food.

No man went hungry in it. I gave to the widow as equally as to her who had a husband. I made no distinction between the great and the small in all I gave. Then came the great inundations, bringers of crops and all things; but I did not exact the arrears of a land-tax.[12]

A Flowering of Arts, Architecture, and Literature

By saving the people in his nome, Amenemhet gained a following of loyal subjects and powerful religious leaders. Although he was not a member of the royal family, he likely exploited his great deeds to gain power and seize the royal throne in a coup around 1994 BC. As pharaoh, Amenemhet I founded the Twelfth Dynasty. Early in his rule he forcibly united Upper and Lower Egypt, which had split during a century of chaos known as the First Intermediate Period.

Amenemhet I's reign marks the beginning of an era of prosperity called the Middle Kingdom, which lasted until about 1640 BC. During this period Egypt experienced a flowering of arts, architecture, and literature, financed in part by an aggressive foreign policy. While Egypt was previously isolated from its neighbors, during the Middle Kingdom Egyptian armies invaded foreign lands and seized wealth and natural resources from the vanquished nations. With a focus on war and conquest, the pharaohs of the Middle Kingdom were often viewed by the people as military leaders with human frailties. This was a departure from the godlike status given to rulers during the Old Kingdom.

Middle Kingdom rulers never had the unquestioned authority of those in previous centuries. This was due to circumstances that began during the Intermediate Period when lack of a central government gave local leaders the freedom to collect taxes and make decisions autonomously. During the Middle Kingdom these lower-level bureaucrats refused to surrender their independence. This proved to be a threat to

The Baffling and Intricate Labyrinth

Amenemhet III's mortuary temple, called the Labyrinth, was described, most likely in exaggerated terms, by Herodotus in the fifth century BC:

> [The labyrinth] has twelve covered courts—six in a row facing north, six south—the gates of the one range exactly fronting the gates of the other, with a continuous wall round the outside of the whole. Inside, the building is of two stories and contains three thousand rooms, of which half are underground, and the other half directly above them. . . . [Of the] upper rooms . . . it is hard to believe that they are the work of men; the baffling and intricate passages from room to room and from court to court were an endless wonder to me, as we passed from a court-yard into rooms, from rooms into galleries, from galleries into more rooms, and thence into yet more courtyards. The roof of every chamber, courtyard, and gallery is, like the walls, of stone. The walls are covered with carved figures, and each court is exquisitely built of white marble and surrounded by a colonnade. Near the corner where the labyrinth ends there is a pyramid, two hundred and forty feet in height, with great carved figures of animals on it and an underground passage by which it can be entered.

Herodotus, *Histories II.* New York: Penguin Classics, 2003, pp. 160–61.

the monarchy and sometimes created political instability. Whereas Old Kingdom rulers were aloof and isolated from day-to-day affairs, Middle Kingdom pharaohs were aggressively political and ever wary of their subordinates.

A New Center of Power

Amenemhet I was aware of his status as an outsider and immediately sought to establish his authority by building a new capital city near present-day Lisht. To ensure his lasting legacy, the pharaoh reminded his subjects that he had united Upper and Lower Egypt, naming the new capital Amenemhet-Itj-Tawy, or "Amenemhet, Seizer of the Two Lands." Itj-Tawy would remain Egypt's capital throughout the Middle Kingdom era.

Itj-Tawy was located at the apex of the Nile delta, the center of power during the Old Kingdom and within sight of the Great Pyramids. Amenemhet I deliberately associated himself with the power and glory of the Old Kingdom by ordering work to begin on his funerary monument, a giant royal pyramid about the same size and form as the Great Pyramid of Giza.

Amenemhet I's pyramid was the first to be built in three centuries. To enhance the importance of the deed, the pharaoh ordered workers to take large blocks of limestone from the Great Pyramid and embed them in the walls of his own tomb. However, the core of the structure of Amenemhet I's pyramid was made of rough blocks of local limestone and filled in with sand and gravel. Mud bricks were laid on top of stone walls. On the outside the pyramid might have resembled the construction marvels of the Old Kingdom, but Amenemhet I's efforts to associate himself with the great pyramid builders of the past were in vain. His monument eventually fell into ruin and today appears as a massive pile of rubble.

Another construction project during the reign of Amenemhet I was undertaken as a foreign policy initiative. Egyptians were long troubled by Bedouin nomads on the northeastern border in present-day Israel who attacked trade caravans. By the time of the Twelfth Dynasty, large numbers of Bedouins were leaving the harsh desert regions in the east to farm the fertile Nile delta. Amenemhet I feared that this migration of foreigners would destabilize Egypt and threaten his power. To prevent such an occurrence, the pharaoh built a massive fortification along Egypt's entire border in the northeastern delta region. Named the "Walls of the Ruler," this giant barricade kept out foreigner invaders for 200 years.

Amenemhet constructed a series of other fortifications and military bases to ensure a steady supply of riches to his royal coffers. Soldiers took control of Nubia, the region along the Nile in southern Egypt and northern Sudan. This move provided access to the Nubian quarries and gold mines. Amenemhet I also extended his reach to the copper and turquoise deposits located in the Sinai Peninsula. In addition, maritime trade routes were strengthened, guaranteeing a steady supply of olive oil, timber, and wine shipped in from the Mediterranean region.

For centuries Egyptians viewed immortality as the province of pharaohs. By the period known as the Middle Kingdom, the general population believed that they too could be granted passage to the afterlife by Osiris, the god of the underworld (pictured here in a tomb painting).

Ameny, the Justified

Despite Amenemhet I's efforts to associate himself with the Old Kingdom, an evolution in religious thinking had forever changed Egypt. People had once believed that the pharaoh, with his godlike status, was the only person who was immortal. However, by the Middle Kingdom, people had come to believe the god Osiris offered immortality to all, regardless of social standing or wealth. This new thinking meant that everyone had access to the afterlife. Every person wanted to be buried with funerary goods. This gave rise to a new Middle Kingdom industry—producing coffins, furniture, canopic jars, statues of deities, and other tomb goods.

Without the support of divine authority for their actions, pharaohs resorted to brute force and intimidation to achieve their goals. In this new setting, political manipulation achieved a new importance, and Amenemhet I was a master of propaganda. He hired scribes to write the "Prophesy of Neferti" to legitimize his dynasty. Although dictated by Amenemhet I, the text claimed to be written during the reign of pharaoh Sneferu during the Fourth Dynasty of the Old Kingdom. In it, social upheaval and disorder is predicted for the Eleventh Dynasty. The chaos is only halted by a divine savior called Ameny, which was Amenemhet I's nickname:

> Then a king will come from the South,
> Ameny, the justified, my name . . .
> He will take the white crown,
> He will join the Two Mighty Ones (the two crowns)
> Asiatics [Bedouins] will fall to his sword,
> Libyans will fall to his flame,
> Rebels to his wrath, traitors to his might,
> As the serpent on his brow subdues the rebels for him,
> One will build the Walls-of-the-Ruler,
> To bar Asiatics from entering Egypt.[13]

Beware of Nobodies

The "Prophesy of Neferti" was written to convince religious and local leaders of Amenemhet I's divine status. Despite this effort at propaganda various monarchs and princes remained powerful, and threatened Amenemhet I's position. In the twentieth year of his reign, to ensure the continuation of his dynasty, Amenemhet I named his son and heir Senusret as coregent, or co-pharaoh. (Senusret is also written as Senuwosret or Sesostris.) Amenemhet I's move to name a coregent was unusual, but it became a regular practice in the centuries that followed. With this move, Egypt had two regents, or rulers, but the effort did little to quell the royal power struggles. In the thirtieth year of Amenemhet I's reign, he was assassinated in his bed by a group of sword-wielding palace insiders. Senusret was in Libya fighting Asiatics but rushed home to take the throne in 1964 BC.

Like his father, Senusret produced propaganda to bolster his reign. The "Instruction of King Amenemhet," written by the scribe Khety, is a fictitious communication from the assassinated pharaoh to his son Senusret:

> Beware of the subjects who are nobodies,
> Of whose plotting one is not aware.
> Do not go near to them alone.
> Trust not a brother, know not a friend,
> Make no intimates, it is worthless.
> When you lie down, guard your heart yourself,
> For no man has adherents on the day of woe.
> I gave to the beggar, I raised the orphan,
> I gave success to the poor as to the wealthy;
> But he who ate my food raised opposition,
> He whom I gave my trust, used it to plot.
> Wearers of my fine linen looked at me as if they were needy,
> Those perfumed with my myrrh poured water while wearing it.[14]

Despite the conditions surrounding his father's demise, the regency of Senusret, from about 1964 to 1929 BC, was peaceful. And like Amenemhet I, the new pharaoh was a great builder, ordering a pyramid constructed near his father's. Senusret also continued the building boom, overseeing construction of numerous shrines, temples, and fortresses throughout Egypt and Nubia.

The prosperity of the Twelfth Dynasty was enhanced by Senusret's grandson, Senusret II, whose coregency and regency lasted from about 1897 to 1878 BC. This pharaoh initiated an enormous irrigation project, diverting a portion of the Nile through a network of canals and dams into the ancient Lake Moeris, about 50 miles (80km) southwest of Memphis. The water turned the shallow swampy lake into the large, fertile Faiyum Oasis, which could now be used for hunting, fishing, irrigation, and water storage in times of drought.

The Labyrinth

The Faiyum Oasis was developed further by the grandson of Senusret II, pharaoh Amenemhet III, who ruled as coregent and regent from approximately 1842 to 1797 BC. Amenemhet III is well known for the building projects he initiated during his reign. He ordered the construction of earthen embankments and a river barrier called a barrage, which greatly expanded the fertile area around Lake Moeris. This work added as many as 17,000 acres (6,879ha) of farmland. To celebrate this accomplishment, the pharaoh erected two colossal statues of himself overlooking the lake at Biyahmu.

Amenemhet III also constructed a brick pyramid by the barrage near Harawa. It contained one of the most elaborate underlying structures of any monument. The burial chamber created to contain the pharaoh's body was carved from a single block of quartzite, the hardest stone available to ancient artisans. The mortuary temple at the pyramid complex was known as the Labyrinth. This was a maze of interconnected galleries filled with precious treasures and astounding artwork. Herodotus wrote about the Labyrinth, "I have seen this building, and it is beyond my power to describe; it must have cost more in labor and money than all the walls and public works of the Greeks put together."[15]

The amazing tomb built by Amenemhet III was actually the second pyramid he ordered. Several years earlier, work began at Dahshur on what was originally called "Amenemhet is Mighty" but is now known

The Black Pyramid at Dahshur (pictured) was abandoned before completion because of water damage. The pyramid was intended to be a grand memorial to Amenemhet III.

as the Black Pyramid for its dark, sad appearance as a mound of rubble. In the early days of construction ground water from the nearby Nile seeped into the pyramid causing structural damage around the foundation. This created massive cracks in chamber walls soon after the pyramid was completed. The pyramid was abandoned before it was finished.

The Terraces of Turquoise

In addition to major construction projects, the era of Amenemhet III is known for the jewelry created by its artisans, which is considered among the finest of ancient Egypt. Jewelers created complex designs using semiprecious stones such as red carnelian, dark blue lapis lazuli, and pale blue turquoise. These stones were inlaid with thin strips of gold into sophisticated pieces. Amenemhet III played an important role in this industry by providing a steady supply of gold and stones to jewelers. This required government-sponsored mining expeditions in some of the harshest deserts in the world.

Conditions in the southwestern Sinai Peninsula, a region called "the Terraces of Turquoise," were particularly severe. In the sixth year of Amenemhet III's reign, a man named Harwerre (also spelled Horwerra) led an expedition of 23 to the terraces. The group consisted of stonecutters, quarrymen, domestic servants, treasury officials, an accountant, a priest, and three cup bearers who fetched water for the others. Harwerre, known by the titles "God's Treasurer" and "Director of Gangs," was a frequent visitor to the turquoise mines. However, this trip was unusual in that it was scheduled for the middle of summer when temperatures could climb as high as 120°F (49°C). The ancient Egyptians erroneously believed that that the quality of turquoise found in the summer was of lower quality. This was the topic of an informal inscription Harwerre carved into a tall sandstone stele, or slab, at the mine. The message, written to bolster the spirits of subsequent miners, has survived intact for more than 3,800 years:

I arrived from Egypt very put out myself, for in my view it would be difficult to find (good) color [of turquoise] while the desert land was hot in the summer, when the mountains burnt (one) and the color was upset. . . . We have commonly heard similarly that raw material is forthcoming at this season of the year, but that color is certainly lacking from it at this miserable time of summer. But I persisted in setting out for this mining land, and my [work] force returned quite complete, without any loss occurring. I was not put out in the face of this labor. . . . I did much more than anyone who had come previously, and much more than all that had been commanded. There was no need for expressions of regret; the color was good . . . [the mine] yielded better than in the regular seasons. . . . I carried out my expedition very well, and no voice was raised against my work, which I executed with success.[16]

Lasting Literature

Harwerre's writing is one example of the many written works produced during the Twelfth Dynasty. This was a time, according to French Egyptologist Nicolas Grimal, "when Egyptian language and literature reached their most perfect forms."[17] The hundreds of surviving manuscripts of the time include political works, religious texts, mythological accounts, and medical and mathematical treatises.

Most papyri are named for the people who purchased or translated them. The *Prisse Papyrus* was obtained by the French Egyptologist Achille Constant Théodore Émile Prisse d'Avennes at Thebes in 1856. The *Prisse Papyrus* contains moral maxims and advice on the practice of virtue. The *Edwin Smith Papyrus*, one of the earliest examples of medical literature, is a textbook on trauma surgery.

The Tale of the Shipwrecked Sailor, written sometime during the Twelfth Dynasty, is one of the oldest surviving narrative tales. This account is told by a sailor who washes up on an island after his ship sinks in the Red Sea. The sailor believes himself fortunate when he finds that the island is flush with food and drink. But then he hears a great rumbling as if the ground is breaking apart, and suddenly a serpent appears. As the sailor peers between the fingers covering his face, he views a serpent 50 feet (15m) long with a beard hanging down to the ground. The serpent's scales are made from gold, and its eyes are glowing lapis lazuli stones. The serpent tells the sailor that he will be rescued in four months and advises him to be brave. The serpent also gives the sailor many gifts including baboons, greyhound dogs, incense, spices, and the ivory tusks of elephants. The sailor returns home and gives the gifts to the pharaoh.

Other great works from the Twelfth Dynasty include mythical stories such as *The Tale of Isis and Ra*, *The Tale of Horus and Seth*, and the legend *The Destruction of Humanity*. The most famous text of the era, however, is the funerary document known as the *Coffin Texts*. Based on the *Pyramid Texts*, written for the royalty of the Old Kingdom, the *Coffin Texts* were updated to provide magical funerary spells for the average person. Any Egyptian who could afford a coffin would hire an artist to paint some of the 1,185 spells in the *Coffin Text* onto his or her casket.

The document known as the *Prisse Papyrus*, dating from the Twelfth Dynasty, is filled with moral maxims such as how to behave while dining. In regular company, the diner should eat little, but in the presence of a glutton, the diner should eat as much as possible.

[In regard to food: abstinence.]

"If thou sittest [at meat] with a company, hate the bread that thou desirest—it is a little moment. Restrain appetite; gluttony is base [shameful]. . . . A cup of water, it quencheth the thirst; a mouthful of melon, it stayeth the appetite. It is a good thing to make substitute for luxury; a little of a small matter can replace a great thing. It is a base fellow who is mastered by his belly . . . free ranging of his belly in their houses.

[When with a great eater or drinker, offend not by over abstinence.]

"If thou sittest at meat with a gormandizer [glutton] . . . if thou drinkest with a toper [drunk] and takest wine, his heart is satisfied. Be not afraid of meat in the company with the greedy; take what he giveth thee; refuse it not, for it will humor him."

Quoted in John W. Cunliffe and Ashley H. Thorndike, eds., *The Warner Library*, vol. 9. New York: Warner Library, 1917, pp. 5327–28.

In the Middle Kingdom era, Osiris was the chief deity of the common people. As such, the *Coffin Texts* focus on the subterranean world, called Duat, ruled by Osiris. Duat, however, is a dangerous place where the dead are faced with many obstacles. Menacing guards stand at the gates of the hereafter. They must be appeased before the dead can enter the afterlife. Other dangers include walls of flame that block the deceased person's path. According to one spell, the corpse of Osiris resides in a region bathed in complete darkness but surrounded by fire. If the deceased can reach this region and look upon Osiris, he or she will achieve immortality.

The Second Intermediate Period

In addition to its literature, jewelry, and astounding monuments, the Twelfth Dynasty is remembered for its royal stability. Pharaohs such as Amenemhet I, Senusret, and Amenemhet III ruled for long periods and provided strong leadership. However, this stability began to break down around 1798 BC when the son of Amenemhet III, Amenemhet IV, assumed the throne for about nine years. Old at the time of his ascension, he was believed to be a weak ruler. Amenemhet IV was replaced by Queen Sobekneferu, possibly his stepsister or aunt. The queen is the first known female pharaoh, but her reign was short, from about 1785 to 1781 BC.

Sobekneferu seemingly had no heirs, and her reign marks the end of the Twelfth Dynasty, an era known as the Golden Age of the Middle Kingdom. The Thirteenth Dynasty, by contrast, is notable for its large number of pharaohs, up to 55, who had brief tenures on the throne. Their names are often obscure, and the exact order and lengths of their reigns is unknown. Unlike rulers from earlier dynasties, these pharaohs were not necessarily related to one another. Historians refer to this era of uncertainty as the Second Intermediate Period. During this era, which lasted from about 1720 to 1550 BC, ancient Egypt fell into disarray much as it had done during the First Intermediate Period.

As the central government dissolved into a rotating group of royal families, bureaucrats, and advisers, the fortresses built during the Twelfth Dynasty deteriorated. In the south, people in the growing Nubian state of Kush were able to evict the Egyptian military leaders that ruled their land. In the north, great numbers of Bedouin immigrants settled around the Faiyum Oasis, and their culture came to dominate the region.

"Chiefs of Foreign Lands"

During the later part of the Thirteenth Dynasty, around 1700 BC, Egypt split once again. While some pharaohs continued to rule from Itj-Tawy, a new set of rulers, those of the Fourteenth Dynasty, came to power in the western part of the Nile delta. Native Egyptians referred to these Asiatic people as *heqa khasewet* or "Chiefs of Foreign Lands." The Greeks later shortened this term to Hyksos. In modern times the foreign invaders are recognized as Arabians from the ancient Middle Eastern lands of Canaan, Aram, Kadesh, Sidon, and Tyre, which lie to the north and east of Egypt.

The Hyksos invaders did not immediately impose their own government on Egypt. Instead they integrated themselves into the ancient political culture already in place. However, the Hyksos forever changed ancient Egypt. The foreigners brought their own customs and traditions to Egypt.

The Hyksos revolutionized warfare with the introduction of body armor and harnessed horses. The foreigners also introduced advanced methods for bronze-working, rebuilt old fortresses, and blazed new trade routes. While the Egyptians did not starve as they had during the First Intermediate Period, the magnificence of the Twelfth Dynasty was gone. For the first time in thousands of years, Egypt was under the control of foreign invaders.

Chapter 4

The New Kingdom

By the 1500s BC the ancient Egyptians had established a culture unlike any other in history. They tamed the Nile, built the Great Pyramids, constructed thousands of other monuments, and created enduring artwork and literature. While these achievements were impressive, Egypt's greatest glories were yet to come. The period known as the New Kingdom, which lasted nearly 500 years from 1550 to 1070 BC, was an era when ancient Egypt expanded its borders into an empire unprecedented in its history. From Central Africa to the Middle East, Egyptian armies conquered territories, pillaged wealth, and extended the powers of famed Eighteenth Dynasty pharaohs such as Thutmose III, Tutankhamen, and Ramses the Great. The New Kingdom rulers used their massive wealth to carve temple complexes from solid stone and stock their burial chambers with glittering treasures.

The wealth, power, and grandeur of the New Kingdom exceeded that of the Middle and Old kingdoms. But like those previous periods of greatness, the New Kingdom grew out of an era marked by suffering and strife.

Pharaoh Crushes Stirrings of Rebellion

The people of Northern Egypt were living through dark days at the end of the sixteenth century BC. Their land was ruled by the pharaoh Apepi, a Hyksos ruler of Syrian heritage. Apepi shared a name with the giant snake that symbolized evil and chaos in Egyptian mythology.

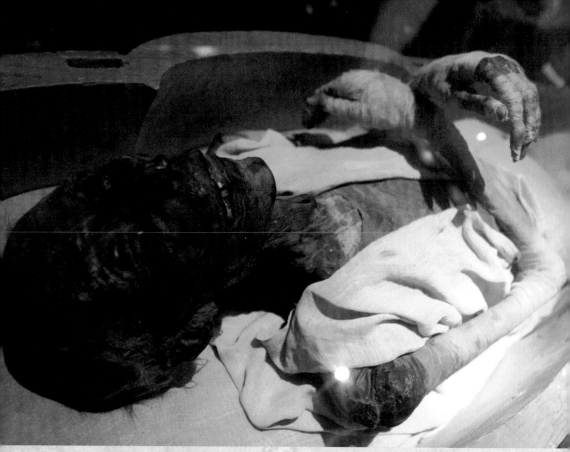

The mummy of Ramses II, also known as Ramses the Great, lies in the Hall of Mummies at Cairo's Egyptian Museum. Ramses II, considered Egypt's last great pharaoh, built magnificent temples and a massive stone statue known as the Colossus of Ramses.

True to his name, Apepi's Fifteenth Dynasty reign was marked by subjugation, oppression, and shame for the Egyptians.

Apepi ruled northern Egypt from the Hyksos capital of Avaris in the northeastern delta. Even though Apepi's strength was in the delta region, those in southern, or Upper Egypt, also had to pay taxes to the Hyksos pharaoh. This provoked rebellious feelings among Egyptians living in the old city of Thebes. Early in Apepi's regency, around 1590 BC, it appeared that the Thebans might threaten the power of the Hyksos pharaoh and topple his government. To prevent any possibility of rebellion Apepi ordered his soldiers to destroy the Theban people and their cherished ancient culture. The historian Manetho described the events in his book *History of Egypt*, written in the third century BC:

The divine anger blew against us, and suddenly . . . [the Hyksos] had the audacity to invade our land. They took possession of it by force, without difficulty and without even having to fight. They captured our leaders, savagely set fire to our cities, and razed the temples of the gods to the ground. They treated the natives with utmost cruelty, cutting the throats of some and taking the wives and children of others as slaves.[18]

Egyptians Throw Off Foreign Rule

Apepi's actions successfully quieted Egyptian opposition for about 20 years. However, around 1574 BC, a brave young Theban ruler named Taa II began a war of liberation against the Hyksos. Taa II was killed trying to conquer Hyksos-controlled territory, but the ruler's son, Kamose, continued the fight.

The exploits of Kamose have been preserved on two stelae installed in the temple of Amun. The temple is located at Karnak, a huge complex of sacred buildings now in ruins near Thebes, or present-day Luxor, about 300 miles (483km) south of Cairo. The words on the stone slabs provide a remarkable description of what was at stake for the Egyptians in their battles against the Hyksos and their Nubian Kush allies.

The narrative begins as Kamose provides the reason for going to war: "No man can settle down when despoiled by the taxes of the Asiatics. I will grapple with him, that I may rip open his belly! My wish is to save Egypt and to smite . . . [Apepi] that Syrian prince with weak arms, who conceives brave things which never come about for him!"[19] The story continues as Kamose describes the spoils of war obtained after he defeated the Hyksos:

Behold! I am come, a successful man! What remains is in my possession, and my venture prospers! . . . Does your heart fail, O you vile Asiatic? Look! I drink of the wine of your vineyards which the Asiatics whom I captured pressed out for me. I have smashed up your resthouse, I have cut down your trees, I have forced your women into ships' holds, I have seized [your] horses; I haven't left a plank to the hundreds of ships of fresh cedar which were filled with gold, lapis, silver, turquoise, bronze axes without number, over and above the . . . oil, incense, fat, honey, willow, box-wood, sticks and all their fine woods—all the fine products . . . I have confiscated all of it! . . . [The] Asiatic has perished![20]

Kamose died suddenly of unknown causes around 1570 BC, but the Egyptian war of liberation continued under his brother, Ahmose I (or Amosis I), founder of the Eighteenth Dynasty. Ahmose I, like Kamose, was a great warrior. He fought in the Battle of Avaris, helping to defeat the Hyksos by sacking their capital city. Pharaoh Ahmose I's army then chased the enemy into Palestine, engaging in a three-year siege against this remaining Hyksos stronghold. According to the pharaoh's biographer, Ahmose I "sailed south to destroy the Nubian Bowmen . . . and made a great slaughter among them."[21]

Ahmose I was viewed as a war hero by the ancient Egyptians. He oversaw the expulsion of the Hyksos and Nubians from Egypt and destroyed the Kush kingdom to the South. Thebes was now the capital of the new, united land. Egypt was freed of foreign rule after more than two centuries of subjugation. This victory and the founding of the Eighteenth Dynasty laid the foundations for the New Kingdom around 1550 BC.

Building an Empire

The long Hyksos occupation taught the ancient Egyptians that they were surrounded by powerful enemies with dangerous armies. Earlier rulers held the belief that the kingdom of Egypt was superior to all others, that it existed at the center of the universe, beyond the reach of invaders. The pharaohs of the Eighteenth Dynasty, however, knew this was not true. As a result, for the first time in Egypt's long history, the kingdom was on a constant war footing with a portion of its great treasure directed towards maintaining a strong

Egyptian Soldiers at War

Ahmose I was a genuine war hero who joined the Egyptian navy while still in his teens. He first served aboard the ship *The Wild Bull*. This vessel was powered by triangular flaxen sails and a team of 30 men who rowed the boat when the winds failed. The ship, filled with troops, weapons, and supplies, patrolled the Nile. When enemies were encountered, soldiers jumped from the ship carrying shields, spears, bows, and bronze-tipped arrows. For protection the soldiers wore body armor consisting of overlapping fabric pads stitched onto leather jackets.

Ahmose I was a skilled bowman. In several battles he attacked Hyksos fortresses with his fellow soldiers, providing a withering hail of arrows upon Egypt's enemies. As the arrows rained down, teams of soldiers scaled the fortifications with ladders. Others splintered the entrance gates with battering rams. When hand-to-hand combat ensued, the infantrymen under Ahmose I's command fought to the death. Whoever prevailed brought the severed hand of his enemy to a scribe who compiled a body count.

standing army. As rulers of a military state, several Eighteenth Dynasty pharaohs in addition to Ahmose I were revered not only as god-kings but as military heroes.

The first great empire builder of the New Kingdom was Thutmose I, whose coronation occurred around 1512 BC. In the second year of his reign the armies of Thutmose I ventured far south into Nubia which was, once again, incorporated into the Egyptian empire. The area, rich in copper and gold, would contribute considerable wealth to the New Kingdom. And Nubia would not regain its independence for another five centuries.

The army of Thutmose I was dominated by soldiers who fought from two-wheel, horse-drawn chariots, which were first introduced by the Hyksos. One soldier drove the chariot, holding up his shield to protect a second man who fired arrows at the enemy. With this fast-moving vehicle of war, the Egyptians swept through Palestine and Syria to the upper Euphrates River.

Expanding Karnak

Thutmose I made Thebes the intellectual and cultural center of the New Kingdom. Memphis, however, was designated the chief headquarters of the military because of its proximity to the newly conquered lands. In the centuries that followed, pharaohs would take their military training in Memphis.

Thutmose I initiated a building boom at the Karnak Temple complex in Thebes. His chief architect Inene was in charge of the extensive construction activity at the temple of Amun where a new building was made for Amun-Re, the god of creation and the patron deity of Thebes.

Amun-Re, or Amun, was believed to be the champion of the poor. This elevated his importance when the Egyptians were repressed by the Hyksos. The stele at Deir el-Medina describes Amun's role:

> You are Amun, the Lord of the silent.
> Who comes at the cry of the poor;
> When I call to you in my distress,
> You come to rescue me.
> Give breath to him who is wretched.
> Rescue me from bondage.
> You are Amun-Re, Lord of Thebes,
> Who rescues him who is in [the netherworld];
> For you are he who is [merciful],
> When one appeals to you.
> You are he who comes from afar.[22]

The pharaohs of the Eighteenth Dynasty attributed their success against the Hyksos to Amun and spared no expense in the construction of the Precinct of Amun-Re at Karnak. The precinct, which occupies 2.6 million square feet (250,000 square m) contains many, temples, towers called pylons, and tall, narrow, four-sided, tapering monuments called obelisks. (Today only the Precinct of Amun-Re is open to visitors. However, the Karnak complex contains three other areas built by later pharaohs, the Precinct of Mut, the Precinct of Montu, and the dismantled Temple of Amenhotep IV.)

Before the work initiated by Thutmose I, the Karnak complex consisted of a long road with a few shrines along it. To celebrate his victory over the Hyksos and honor Amun-Re, the powerful pharaoh drastically enlarged the complex, erecting pylons and a pair of obelisks carved from red granite. In addition, Inene oversaw construction of a large hall, several colossal statues, and giant stone columns.

During the next two dynasties, pharaohs expanded the Karnak complex, each adding a room or hall to the Amun temple. Every project featured intricately carved hieroglyphic inscriptions on nearly every wall and pillar. Much of what is known today about the New Kingdom comes from the stories told by these inscriptions.

The Valley of the Kings

In addition to expanding Karnak's boundaries, Thutmose I was the first known pharaoh to build his tomb in what is referred to today as the Valley of the Kings because of the number of pharaohs entombed there. This barren valley located on the west bank of the Nile lay hidden behind steep cliffs and was difficult to access on foot. Thutmose I selected the valley for its isolation. He was aware that pyramids built by previous pharaohs had been plundered by grave robbers who stole valuable treasures left in the tombs. Inene noted Thutmose I's tomb would be safe, writing, "I saw to the excavation of the rock-tomb of his majesty, alone, no one seeing, no one hearing."[23]

Thutmose I was entombed upon his death in 1518 BC, and the Valley of the Kings received the bodies of the New Kingdom pharaohs for the next 450 years. The valley contains at least 63 tombs including those of favored nobles. The burial site's importance is denoted by its

1 Ramses VII

2 Ramses IV

3 Son of Ramses III

46 Yuya and Tuya

4 Ramses XI

62 Tutankhamen

7 Ramses II

8 Merenptah

5 Sons of Ramses II

6 Ramses IX

9 Ramses V/VI

55 Tiy

Rest-house

57 Horemheb

12

58 56

45 Userhet

44 Tentkaru

35 Amenhotep II

48 Amenhotep I

53

11

Ramses III

17 Sety I

54

28

27

21

36 Maiherpri

61

16 Ramses I

10 Amenmesse

18 Ramses X

20 Hatshepsut

13 Bey

29

60

47 Siptah

14 Twosret/Sethnakht

40

38 Thutmose I

26

30

59

43 Thutmose IV

15 Sety II

31

19 Mentuherkepshef

32

37

42 Thutmose II or Wife of Thutmose III

33

34 Thutmose III

82 yards
(75m)

official name in ancient times, "The Great and Majestic Necropolis of the Millions of Years of the Pharaoh, Life, Strength, Health in the West of Thebes."

Like Thutmose I, the pharaohs later buried in the Valley of the Kings were placed in deep tombs cut into the rocks. Typical layouts consisted of long sloping corridors that descended through one or more halls to the burial chamber. After a pharaoh's mummy was placed in the chamber, the halls were filled with rubble and the entrance to the site hidden beneath sand and rocks.

Like all royal tombs in ancient Egypt, those in the Valley of the Kings were filled with funerary texts and pictures. These texts include the *Book of the Dead* and the *Book of Gates*, which describe the pharaoh's journey into the next world. The *Book of Gates* describes the gates the soul must pass through on different parts of the journey to the afterlife. Each gate is ruled by a specific goddess, and the dead must recognize and honor her before passing to the next gate. Those who are morally upright may pass unharmed, those with evil in their hearts will fall into a lake of fire.

Later during the New Kingdom, the wives and children of pharaohs were buried in the nearby Valley of the Queens. The tombs in both valleys, however, did not remain secret. They were plundered by thieves throughout history, except for Tutankhamen's tomb, which was discovered completely intact in the twentieth century AD.

Queen Hatshepsut

Thutmose I died around 1518 BC and was replaced by his son Thutmose II. The new pharaoh was married to his half-sister, Hatshepsut, and the two ruled Egypt as coregents. A stele in the tomb of Inene describes Hatshepsut's role in the government: "Thutmose I went up to heaven and was united with the gods. His son took his place as King of the Two Lands. . . . His sister, the God's Wife Hatshepsut, dealt with the affairs of state; the Two Lands were under her government and taxes were paid to her."[24]

Thutmose II and Hatshepsut ruled as coregents for about 14 years. In 1504 BC, Thutmose II, who was in his early thirties, died.

Before his death he named his son, Thutmose III, as pharaoh. However, Thutmose III was a young boy, and Hatshepsut refused to relinquish her power. In 1498 BC, Hatshepsut had herself crowned as the one and only pharaoh. In order to justify her coup, she claimed that her coregent was not Thutmose III but her deceased father Thutmose I. Like previous pharaohs, Hatshepsut created propaganda to solidify her position. The texts are written on the walls of her mortuary temple beneath the cliffs at Deir el Bahari on the west bank of the Nile near the Valley of the Kings. The work is both a political and mythological story that states that the birth of Hatshepsut was overseen by the god Amun himself. The revered deity also oversaw her education. The story continues, "After being proclaimed king by the gods, she must still be crowned by mankind. Her human father, Thutmose I, introduces her to the royal court, nominates her, and has her acclaimed as heir."[25]

Hatshepsut, who ruled successfully for 15 peaceful years, was one of ancient Egypt's most productive builders. Working with Inene, she enlarged the Karnak Precinct of Mut, which was dedicated to the Egyptian mother goddess Mut, and oversaw installation of two huge obelisks that, at the time, were the tallest in the world.

Epic Battles

Upon Hatshepsut's death in 1483 BC, Thutmose III once again became pharaoh. The third Thutmose had been kept from his rightful place on the throne for nearly two decades by the powerful Hatshepsut. Historians speculate he might have participated in a plot to poison her. While this is speculation, it is known that Thutmose III destroyed many of the records describing the glorious deeds of the queen.

The ambitious Thutmose III was determined to outdo all his predecessors in terms of foreign policy. During the pharaoh's 54-year reign he was the strongest military leader to ever lead Egypt, creating the largest empire in Egyptian history.

The annals of Thutmose III's epic battles are inscribed on temple walls at Karnak. They make up the longest, most detailed historical

The deceased sails through the underworld on his journey to the afterlife in this panel from the Book of the Dead. *The royal tombs in the Valley of the Kings were filled with funerary texts and pictures such as this one.*

records about ancient Egypt to have survived to modern times. In the first 20 years of his regency, Thutmose III oversaw 17 military campaigns from the Euphrates to Nubia. More than 350 cities were captured and plundered by Egyptian soldiers.

The treasures obtained during these campaigns brought great wealth to Thutmose III. He used the riches to fund an extensive building program throughout his growing empire. By the time of his death, around 1450 BC, Egypt controlled a vast swath of territory from the banks of the Euphrates to southern Nubia. Such power would never again be matched, and the deeds of Thutmose III were celebrated and honored for 1,500 years after his death.

The One and Only God

The empire built by early Eighteenth Dynasty pharaohs remained rich and powerful for decades. However, around 1350 BC, there was great turmoil within the kingdom. Amenhotep IV was the pharaoh, and during the fifth year of his reign the ruler took a new name and attempted to change Egyptian religious beliefs and practices. Amenhotep became Effective Spirit of Aten, or Akhenaten. Aten was a manifestation of the ancient sun god Ra-Harakhte. While Ra had been the supreme god of Egypt for millennia, Amun had taken his place in the New Kingdom. Akhenaten not only elevated Aten to supremacy, he claimed that the deity was the one and only god, above all other deities. The pharaoh stated this in a poem he wrote called "Great Hymn to the Aten":

> How manifold it is, what thou hast made!
> They are hidden from the face (of man).
> O sole god, like whom there is no other!
> Thou didst create the world according to thy desire.[26]

Ancient Egyptians were polytheistic, meaning they believed in many gods; they worshipped dozens of gods. Akhenaten overturned centuries of religious belief and practice by proclaiming the existence of only one god and by banning the worship of all others. Akhenaten's actions affected all areas of art, government, and religion. To carry out this revolutionary reorganization of Egyptian culture, the pharaoh employed teams of civil officials from the lower classes and even foreign nations. Driven by religious zealotry, these officials used chisels and knives to systematically eradicate any mention of Amun on obelisks, stelae, columns, statues, and temple walls. Lesser gods were also removed. At the same time, Akhenaten elevated himself as the sole intermediary between Aten and his people, eliminating the traditional role of priests. His followers worshipped him as both god and prophet.

King Tut Restores Order

When Akhenaten died around 1334 BC, Tutankhamen ascended to the throne. The new pharaoh, who was the child of Akhenaten and

King Tut's Tomb

Tutankhamen is one of the most famous Egyptian kings because his tomb was the richest of the few royal burial chambers that survived intact to the modern age. Tut's tomb was hidden by rock chips dumped from cutting the tomb of a later king. In 1922 Egyptologist Howard Carter discovered the four-room tomb, which was jam-packed with 3,000 extraordinary treasures, including a solid gold coffin, a gold mask, an ivory-and-gold-encrusted throne, and gold jewelry. Tutankhamen was entombed with various pieces of furniture including three couches carved into animal shapes, chests, chairs, and stools. For sport in the afterlife, Tutankhamen had a chariot, 130 walking sticks, 46 bows, 400 arrows, clubs, boomerangs, and knives. To clothe himself in the afterlife, King Tut was equipped with sandals, necklaces, mirrors, slippers decorated with gold, linen loincloths, and 27 pairs of embroidered gloves. In the way of food, Tutankhamen was buried with 11 baskets of watermelon seeds and 30 large jars of vintage wine.

one of the pharaoh's sisters, was only nine years old when he came to power. The young pharaoh had strong advisers who took control of the government. During Tutankhamen's short reign, Amun was restored as supreme deity, and a new temple was built to the god at Karnak.

Tutankhamen died at age 19 and was buried in the Valley of the Kings. His reign occurred during a period of decline of the Eighteenth Dynasty. Priests who were dedicated to other deities and persecuted under Akhenaten sought to strengthen their positions in society so they would not lose power again. This created a situation where priests and religious cults were battling one another for power and wealth.

Ramses the Great

While preoccupied with the internal struggles of the Eighteenth Dynasty, Egypt ignored its foreign outposts. That changed with Ramses II, or Ramses the Great, who ascended the throne in 1279 BC. Ramses II ruled for 67 years and is counted as the last great pharaoh of ancient Egypt. During the period of his reign, Ramses II led military campaigns in Syria, Libya, and Nubia, conquering all of Egypt's neighbors. After subjugating the people, the pharaoh married royal princesses from each country. This helped erase hard feelings between former enemies, creating instead strong alliances based on royal marriage. The joining of royal houses also ensured a steady flow of riches from the conquered lands to the imperial coffers.

Ramses II used this wealth to create huge statues, temples, and other buildings that are the hallmark of his reign. Among the structures are two magnificent temples at Abu Simbel in Nubia and the Hypostyle Hall at Karnak, which historians consider one of the world's greatest architectural masterpieces. In addition, the pharaoh ordered the Colossus of Ramses at Memphis. This massive stone statue is almost 39 feet long (10m). It is so intricately carved that modern sculptors still puzzle over the processes used to make it. Sculptor Stuart M. Edelson was unable to recreate a similar statue using modern tools. He says, "How these master carvers achieved perfect surfaces on this scale with simple tools was beyond my comprehension. My own twenty years' experience provided no clue."[27]

Unrest and Foreign Rule

Ramses the Great lived to be 96 years old—far older than the average person of the time. He had 200 wives and concubines, 96 sons, and 60 daughters. His Colossus, like the pyramids and countless other creations of the ancient Egyptians, continues to astound thousands of years after its creation. However, after the Nineteenth Dynasty ended in 1187 BC, the magnificence of ancient Egypt would never again be matched. During the Twentieth Dynasty, Egyptians experienced years of drought that dried up the Nile. This resulted in bad harvests, starva-

tion, and civil unrest. Egypt's weakness was heightened by official cor-
ruption and internal power struggles. These pressures brought the end
of the New Kingdom around 1064 BC. The Third Intermediate Period
that followed was a time of foreign rule. During this period, Egyptians continued to worship their traditional gods and build temples
and tombs, but their ancient culture began to disappear.

Egypt's Late Period, from 664 to 323 BC, was dominated by the
cultural influences of Greece, Rome, and Persia (present-day Iran). In
332 BC, Greek king Alexander the Great conquered Egypt, and Egyptians would not control their country again until the 1900s. The great
age of ancient Egypt, which had lasted nearly 3000 years, was swept
aside with the drifting sands of the desert.

Chapter 5

What Is the Legacy of Ancient Egypt?

In 1886 the renowned British scholar and diplomat Richard Burton wrote that ancient Egypt was "the inventor of the alphabet, the cradle of letters . . . [and] generally, the source of all human civilization."[28] When Burton made this statement new discoveries were being made about ancient Egypt every year. Scholars were translating hieroglyphs, and archeologists were unearthing treasure-laden tombs. This work made it increasingly clear that the ancient Egyptians helped build the foundation of Western thought and culture.

This process of transferring ancient Egyptian knowledge to the West began around the seventh century BC. At that time scholars of classical Greece, also called Hellenistic culture, became eager students of ancient Egyptian concepts concerning religion, philosophy, medicine, astrology, art, and architecture. As Professor Emeritus of Ancient History Stanley Burstein explains, "references to Egypt and its culture occur in the works of almost every . . . classical [Greek] author."[29] The Egyptian ideas adapted by the Greeks were later incorporated into Roman culture, which influenced European thought and society well into the modern age.

Egyptian Mathematics

The Egyptians were among the world's earliest master mathematicians. They invented symbols for numerals and perfected addition, subtraction, multiplication, division, and fractions as well as geometry and algebra. These concepts were put to work for land-surveying, building irrigation systems along the Nile, and designing and constructing incredibly complex buildings such as the pyramids. The classical Greeks learned many mathematical concepts, such as geometry and algebra, from ancient Egypt. The Greeks improved on these mathematical sciences, perfected them, and shaped them into their present forms.

Many classical Greek mathematicians, including Thales, Pythagoras, Plato, and Archimedes, were said to have studied in Egypt. Pythagoras, born in 560 BC, is responsible for developing important theories about numbers, geometry, philosophy, and science. The Pythagorean theorem, which provides a formula to measure a triangle, is a basic concept of geometry. While no writings by Pythagoras exist, the mathematician is commonly believed to have spent more than two decades studying in Egypt, as Greek scholar Iamblichus wrote in the fourth century BC:

> [Pythagoras] studied with the priests and prophets and instructed himself on every possible topic, neglecting no . . . rite practiced in the country wherever it was, and leaving no place unexplored where he thought he could discover something more. . . . And so he spent 22 years in the shrines throughout Egypt, pursuing astronomy and geometry and . . . all the rites of divine worship. . . . [He] attained to the highest eminence in arithmetic, music, and the other branches of learning.[30]

At the age of 56 Pythagoras returned to Greece, where his theories about geometry and philosophy, influenced by the Egyptians, were adopted by influential scholars such as Plato, Aristotle, and Euclid. Plato himself studied in Egypt for 13 years, and some believe that he copied ancient mathematical concepts directly from ancient Egyptian papyri into his own writings around 360 BC.

Adopting Egyptian Gods

While Pythagoras, Plato, and other Greek scholars were studying in Egypt they participated in Egyptian religious rites and studied ancient

The Pyramid on the Dollar Bill

The US one dollar bill is one of the most recognizable currencies in the world. Among the many items pictured on the dollar, the Great Seal of the United States has roots in ancient Egypt. The back of the Great Seal, on the left side of the dollar, shows an unfinished or uncapped pyramid. This symbol is modeled on the Great Pyramid of Giza. Hovering above the symbol is the capstone, or top part, which, if lowered, would complete the pyramid. Inside the capstone is an eye, called the Eye of Providence, surrounded by rays of light. The Eye of Providence is based on the ancient Egyptian Eye of Ra, also known as the Eye of Horus. It is an ancient Egyptian symbol of protection and divine royal power. The Eye is considered the all-seeing eye and protects the king and thwarts all evil.

religious philosophy. During Alexander's rule of Hellenistic Egypt, the Greeks began to worship major Egyptian deities, and they began merging them with several of their own important gods. The great messenger god of Greek mythology, Hermes, was linked to Thoth, one of the chief deities of the Egyptian pantheon. Both Thoth and Hermes were gods of writing and magic, in charge of guiding souls to the afterlife. Together they were known in Hellenistic Egypt as Hermes Trismegistus. (Trismegistus means thrice or three-times great, although the origins of this name are unknown.)

A book called *The Emerald Tablet of Hermes Trismegistus* contains writings attributed to the god Hermes Trismegistus. In the text Hermes discusses ancient Egyptian concepts of religion and magic, which were mixed with beliefs about astrology. The Egyptians believed that the moon, sun, planets, and stars were living gods responsible for all life on Earth. These important cosmic deities were able to see into the future and reveal messages about the destiny of mortals. The ancient Egyptian belief in astrology was described by the historian Diodorus of Sicily around 60 BC:

> The positions and arrangements of the stars, as well as their motion, have always been the subject of careful observations among the Egyptians. . . . And while [the stars] often succeed in predicting to men the events that will befall them in the course of their lives, not infrequently they foretell destruction of the crops, or, on the other hand, abundant yields, and pestilences . . . [and the stars] have prior knowledge of earthquakes and floods, and the risings of comets, and of all things which the ordinary man regards as quite beyond finding out.[31]

The ancient Egyptian belief that the stars could predict a person's future was central to Hermetic thinking and adopted by the Greeks. This could be seen in the importance given to horoscopes in Hellenistic society. When a baby was born, astrologers determined the exact location of the sun, moon, and planets in relation to the zodiac at that moment. This would determine a child's birth sign such as Virgo, Scorpio, and so on. The birth horoscope was used throughout the rest of a person's life to make predictions about important decisions. The astrological concepts pioneered by the ancient Egyptians and adapted by the Greeks remain popular today.

Renaissance Thinkers Rediscover Ancient Egypt

The classical Greeks had an intense interest in ancient Egyptian concepts such as astrology and magic. However, the culture of the pharaohs was largely forgotten after Egypt became a province of the Roman Empire around 30 BC. When the emperor Constantine made Christianity the official religion of the Roman Empire in AD 380, many Egyptians converted to Christianity. During this time, indigenous knowledge of ancient Egyptian religion died out as did the understanding of the hieroglyphics. However, during the Italian Renaissance, around AD 1460, the writings of Hermes Trismegistus were translated from Greek to Italian. Renaissance scholars rediscovered this collection of mystical writings and viewed the work as wisdom from the time of the pharaohs.

Interest in the religion, magic, and astrology of Hermiticism sparked a widespread interest in all things Egyptian. Renaissance intellectuals focused their interest on ancient Egyptian artwork, statues, jewelry, and sculptures. In the mid-1400s, this interest set the stage for the emergence of what was called an "Egyptian revival" in Rome. During this revival, obelisks, pyramids, and ancient Egyptian artwork were placed in and around the most important buildings in Italy, including the Vatican, which housed the central governing body of Christianity. Pope Nicholas V initiated the Egyptian revival around 1450 when he raised a massive Egyptian-style obelisk in the plaza in front of the Vatican.

In 1492 Pope Alexander VI hired the painter named Bernadino di Betto to paint six rooms at the Vatican, known as the Appartamenti Borgia, with scenes from Egyptian antiquity. These paintings told the stories of Osiris, Isis, and the sacred bull Apis. The works were meant to express Pope Alexander VI's contention that he was a direct descendent of the sun god Osiris. The Egyptian revival continued under Leo X, who was pope from 1513 to 1521. In 1517, Pope Leo installed two black Egyptian sphinx statues on the steps of one of the most important buildings in Rome, the Palace of the Senate, where the central government met. The marble sphinx statues were carved during the Twenty-Ninth Dynasty and brought to Italy in the Middle Ages.

A Craze for Egyptology

The Egyptian revival inspired traders to bring shiploads of plundered goods from Egyptian temples and tombs back to Europe. By the end of the eighteenth century, the desire for Egyptian artifacts reached a peak. Perhaps no European was as fascinated by ancient Egypt as the French general Napoléon Bonaparte. When Napoléon invaded Egypt with 54,000 soldiers on July 1, 1798, he brought along 167 savants, or technical experts, including scientists, engineers, and archeologists. During

THE JUNE CENTURY

NAPOLEON IN EGYPT

Ancient Egypt fascinated France's Napoléon Bonaparte. When his troops invaded Egypt in 1798 he brought along more than a hundred scientists, engineers, and archaeologists to study what remained of Egypt's ancient civilization.

the next several years the scholars conducted investigations into Egypt's natural history, geography, technology, chemistry, and medicine. The main focus, however, was on Egypt's past. Archeological expeditions and scientific studies were conducted at some of the most renowned ruins, such as Karnak and Thebes. The work was cataloged in the encyclopedic *Description de l'Égypte,* which contains over 3,000 illustrations including detailed drawings of tombs, temples, and other ruins.

Description de l'Égypte became a best seller and ignited a craze for Egyptology. After reading the book, travelers from across the globe made plans to visit Egypt and dig for treasures. At the time there were no laws against looting. Professional excavators descended on ancient monuments and dug up priceless artifacts for sale to museums and wealthy patrons.

The Rosetta Stone

Napoléon's military invasion was ultimately a failure, and the French left Egypt in 1801. However, an accidental discovery by the French military forever changed the way the world understood ancient Egypt. In 1799 soldiers were digging up stones to reinforce coastal fortifications in the town of Rosetta on the Nile delta. The soldiers discovered a black basalt stone inscribed with three horizontal panels of text. What came to be called the Rosetta Stone was turned over to archeologists at the Institute of Egypt, an organization founded by Napoléon in Cairo in 1798 to promote study of ancient Egypt.

Scholars at the Institute of Egypt recognized the importance of the Rosetta Stone almost immediately. The inscriptions were written in two languages and three scripts—hieroglyphs, a form of Arabic, and ancient Greek. It was understood that the three texts contained the same content. Translation of the Greek letters revealed the inscription was a decree issued in Memphis in 196 BC by King Ptolemy V, the fifth ruler of the Hellenistic Ptolemaic Dynasty. This dynasty ruled Egypt from 305 BC to 30 BC.

The Rosetta Stone was originally part of a stele displayed in a temple. It was moved for unknown reasons to its resting place near Rosetta. After its discovery, hundreds of linguists studied the inscription on the stone.

Attempts to decipher the hieroglyphs on the Rosetta Stone were largely unsuccessful. However, in 1822 French scholar and linguist Jean-François Champollion cracked the code. Champollion, born in 1790, was fascinated by hieroglyphs as a young boy and planned to spend his life unlocking the secrets of the ancient Egyptian alphabet. To do so, he learned to speak Hebrew, Arabic, Latin, and Greek by the time he was 17.

In 1820, after studying the Rosetta Stone for years, Champollion concluded that the hieroglyphs were a combination of symbols. Some represented phonetic sounds, others ideas. This meant only certain symbols were meant to be read as words while others stood for concepts like king or god. After Champollion announced his discovery on September 27, 1822, others were able to understand the ancient Egyptian writing system. In the years that followed, the long-hidden secrets of the pharaoh's people were revealed.

Ancient Medicine

After Champollion deciphered the hieroglyphs, a much clearer picture emerged of daily life in ancient Egypt. Scholars have come to understand, for instance, that the Egyptians had a highly evolved understanding of the human body and its various diseases and afflictions. This information was revealed in a number of papyri dedicated to medical problems and cures.

The *Edwin Smith Papyrus* is the world's oldest surviving medical textbook. The papyrus, taken from the tomb of a physician, is dated 1550 BC and has 32 pages. The text contains information about serious injuries to the throat and neck, collarbone, arms, chest, and wounds to the face. Some treatments in the papyrus remained in use for thousands of years. For example, the writer suggests binding a broken bone with splints held in place by strips of cloth bandages.

The Smith papyrus contains practical information to cure the wounded. However, many other medical texts of the time rely on

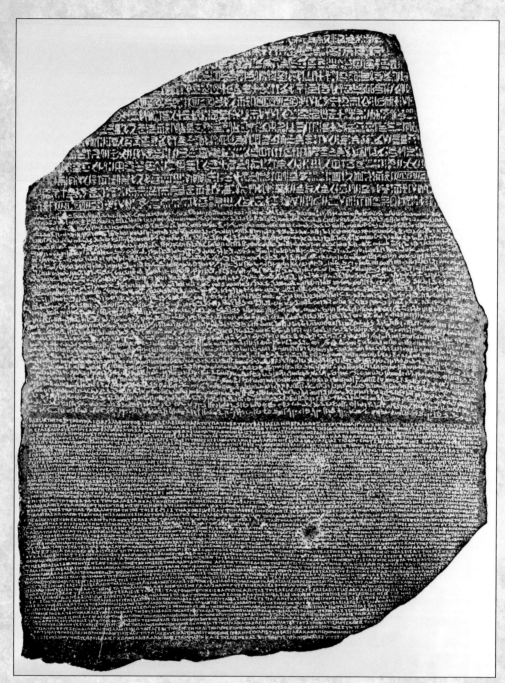

While digging for stones to reinforce fortifications, Napoléon's soldiers dug up a black basalt stone inscribed with three horizontal panels of text. The text of the Rosetta Stone, pictured here in a display at the British Museum, praises and honors pharaohs.

spells, chants, and magical rituals for healing. The *Ebers Medical Papyrus*, translated in 1890, contains many charms and invocations to encourage healing. One spell, recited before taking an herbal concoction, reads, "Come Remedy! Come thou who expellest [evil] things in this my stomach and in these my limbs! The spell is powerful over the remedy. Repeat it backwards! Really excellent, [proved] many times!"[32]

While the chants and charms may have been ineffective, the Egyptians understood the power of herbal medicine. Doctors ordered those with asthma and other bronchial problems to eat raw garlic mixed with oils and herbs. Garlic was also mixed with vinegar and used as a gargle to treat toothaches and sore throats. Onions were recommended for digestive ailments. Leaves of coriander were made into tea for urinary complaints, and cumin was applied to joints to relieve the pain of arthritis.

The ancient Egyptian knowledge of anatomy and medicine was passed down to the Greeks and Arabs who were famous for their medical skills. Plant-based curatives from the time of the pharaohs were used throughout the world for thousands of years. Even after the advent of modern medicine in the twentieth century, belief in herbal medicine remained strong. In the twenty-first century hundreds of herbal remedies are sold in drug stores and health food stores. Some of these products contain herbal concoctions that might have been familiar to a doctor practicing medicine in ancient Egypt.

Architectural Influence

Perhaps the most tangible influence of ancient Egypt is in the architectural designs still used today throughout the world. Like many other aspects of antique cultural influence, Egyptian building designs were first adapted by Greek architects during the Hellenist era.

Classical Greek architectural styles are named for the types of columns used in construction. These column designs were copied from ancient Egyptian temples, palaces, and monuments. The ancient Egyptian column consists of three parts. A pedestal is at the bottom of each column, the tapering column itself is in the middle, and a crown called a capital is at the top of the column. In Egypt the crown was often carved with intricate designs such as bundles of papyrus.

The Greeks took Egyptian column designs and used them to develop three orders of architecture, Doric, Ionic, and Corinthian. These styles are based on the shape and size of the columns. The fluted Doric column designs, first seen in Egyptian temples, were used to construct the famous Greek Parthenon in Athens around 447 BC. This classical column style was later used in Roman architecture and may be seen today in thousands of building throughout the world.

Some of the most famous landmarks in Washington, DC, have architectural features similar to buildings in ancient Egypt. The Lincoln Memorial, finished in 1922, is patterned after an Egyptian temple honoring the pharaoh Ramses II. At the Lincoln Memorial, a large granite statue of the sixteenth president, Abraham Lincoln, is housed in a structure built with 36 Doric columns.

Obelisks and Pyramids

The design of another presidential monument in Washington has roots in ancient Egypt. The Washington Monument, completed in 1888, is the world's tallest obelisk, standing over 555 feet (169m) high. Obelisks are prominent features at the Karnak temple complex where five of the original 13 structures remain standing today. The Washington Monument was designed in the 1840s by architect Robert Mills who acknowledged the ancient influence by placing a relief of an Egyptian winged disc above a carving of George Washington in the entryway.

The Washington Monument serves the same purpose as an ancient Egyptian obelisk. The original obelisks were erected to proclaim the power and success of a ruler. The Washington Monument stands as a symbol of George Washington's contribution to the United States and the tribute its citizens pay to the first president. The vault where Washington is buried is framed by two obelisks, and the graves of two other presidents, Thomas Jefferson and James Madison, are marked by large obelisk tombstones.

Pioneers in Medicine

The *Ebers Medical Papyrus* is one of the earliest books of surgery in the world, describing 48 surgical cases of traumatic nature. Many concepts about the human body described in the papyrus are very accurate and have formed the basis for modern medical treatment. Each case begins with a quick diagnosis followed by a detailed diagnosis, a clear prognosis, and therapy to cure the problem. In the papyrus, doctors explain how to set fractured bones in plaster casts, apply splints, and suture wounds. They also explain that blood vessels lead to every part of the body and describe the relationship of the heart to the circulation of the blood. The effectiveness of ancient Egyptian medicine has been proved by archeologists examining mummified remains of pharaohs. Many have been found with perfectly healed fractures and other signs of expert medical care.

Pyramids have also been used on countless tombs, monuments, and buildings throughout history. In the first century AD, the Romans built the Pyramid of Cestius to honor Caius Cestius, a wealthy magistrate. Pyramids were later built in Greece, France, and Spain, but the modern age of pyramid building did not begin in earnest until the last decades of the twentieth century. While modern pyramids cannot compare to those of ancient Egypt, several were designed by one of the century's most famous architects, I.M. Pei. He designed the 70-foot-high Louvre Pyramid (26m) in front of the famed Louvre Palace art museum in Paris, France. The large steel-and-glass pyramid, built in 1989, is surrounded by three smaller pyramids. Clearly, the structure owes its design to the Great Pyramid of Giza. Pei also designed another famous pyramid, the steel and glass structure that houses the Rock and Roll Hall of Fame, which opened in 1995 in Cleveland, Ohio.

The Immortal Egyptians

Like the pyramids at Giza, the philosophy, astronomy, medicine, and art of ancient Egypt continues to influence modern society. Perhaps the ancient Egyptians were correct in their belief that magical texts and tombs would provide them immortality. More than 2,000 years after the fall of the pharaohs, people continue to discuss their world, thoughts, and creative endeavors. In this way, the ancient Egyptians have lived on.

Source Notes

Chapter One: What Conditions Led to the Rise of Ancient Egypt?

1. Quoted in Leland M. Roth, *Understanding Architecture: Its Elements, History, and Meaning*. Boulder, CO: Westview, 1993, p. 188.
2. Barbara Mertz, *Temples, Tombs, & Hieroglyphs: A Popular History of Ancient Egypt*. New York: HarperCollins, 2007, p. 13.
3. Cyril Aldred, *Egypt to the End of the Old Kingdom*. New York: McGraw-Hill, 1965, p. 42.
4. Quoted in Aldred, *Egypt to the End of the Old Kingdom*, p. 45.

Chapter Two: The Pyramid Age

5. Quoted in Miriam Lichtheim, *Ancient Egyptian Literature: A Book of Readings*, vol. 1. Berkeley: University of California Press, 1973, pp. 41–42.
6. Quoted in Charlotte Booth, *People of Ancient Egypt*. Stroud, UK: Tempus, 2006, p. 22.
7. Herodotus, *Histories II*. New York: Penguin Classics, 2003, p. 124.
8. Robert Bauval and Adrian Gilbert, *The Orion Mystery: Unlocking the Secrets of the Pyramids*. New York: Crown, 1994, pp. 42–43.
9. Bauval and Gilbert, *The Orion Mystery*, p. 44.
10. Quoted in Mertz, *Temples, Tombs, & Hieroglyphs*, p. 96.

Chapter Three: The Middle Kingdom

11. Quoted in T.G.H. James, *Pharaoh's People*. London: I.B. Tauris, 2003, pp. 113–14.
12. Quoted in James, *Pharaoh's People*, p. 113.
13. Quoted in Ivan Van Sertima, ed., *Egypt Revisited*, vol. 10. New Brunswick: Transaction, 1989, p. 218.

14. Quoted in Nicolas Grimal, *A History of Ancient Egypt*. Oxford, UK: Blackwell, 1994, p. 163.

15. Herodotus, *Histories II*, p. 156.

16. Quoted in James, *Pharaoh's People*, p. 39.

17. Grimal, *A History of Ancient Egypt*, p. 171.

Chapter Four: The New Kingdom

18. Quoted in Pierre Montet, *Lives of the Pharaohs*. Cleveland: World Publishing, 1968, p. 68.

19. Quoted in James B. Pritchard, ed., *Ancient Near Eastern Texts*, vol. 1. Princeton: Princeton University Press, 1969, pp. 232–33.

20. Quoted in E.D. Oren, ed., *The Hyksos: New Historical and Archaeological Perspectives*. Philadelphia: University of Pennsylvania Museum Publication, 1997, p. 1.

21. Quoted in Stefan G. Chrissanthos, *Warfare in the Ancient World: From the Bronze Age to the Fall of Rome*. Westport, CT: Praeger, 2008, p. 3.

22. Quoted in Miriam Lichtheim, *Ancient Egyptian Literature: The New Kingdom*, vol. 2. Berkeley: University of California Press, 1976, p. 106.

23. Quoted in Arthur E.P. Weigall, *A Guide to the Antiquities of Upper Egypt: From Abydos to the Sudan Frontier*. New York: Macmillan, 1910, p. 196.

24. Quoted in Grimal, *A History of Ancient Egypt*, p. 207.

25. Quoted in Grimal, *A History of Ancient Egypt*, p. 209.

26. Quoted in Pritchard, *Ancient Near Eastern Texts*, p. 227.

27. Quoted in John Anthony West, *The Traveler's Key to Ancient Egypt: A Guide to the Sacred Places of Ancient Egypt*. Wheaton, IL: Quest, 1995, p. 194.

Chapter Five: What Is the Legacy of Ancient Egypt?

28. Richard Burton, *The Book of the Thousand Nights and a Night*, vol. 6. Charleston, SC: BiblioBazaar, pp. 382–83.

29. Quoted in Brian Curran, *The Egyptian Renaissance: The Afterlife of Ancient Egypt in Early Modern Italy.* Chicago: University of Chicago Press, 2007, p. 16.

30. Quoted in Thomas Little Heath, *A History of Greek Mathematics: From Thales to Euclid*, vol. 1. Mineola, NY: Dover, 1981, p. 5.

31. Diodorus Siculus, *The Library of History.* Cambridge, MA: Loeb Classical Library, 1933, p. 279.

32. Quoted in Plinio Prioreschi, *A History of Medicine*, vols. 1, 2. Omaha: Horatius, 1999, p. 308.

Important People of Ancient Egypt

Alexander the Great: Alexander was a Greek king who created one of the largest empires in the ancient world. He conquered Egypt in 332 BC, ending thousands of years of reign by the pharaohs.

Amenhotep IV or Akhenaten: After ascending to the throne in 1350 BC the pharaoh changed his name to Effective Spirit of Aten, or Akhenaten. His reign was marked by religious turmoil as he zealously elevated the sun Aten to supremacy while banning worship of Amun and numerous other religious deities.

Djoser: When Djoser became the second pharaoh of the Third Dynasty he ordered construction of the first of the pyramids, the Step Pyramid at Saqqara.

Hatshepsut: Queen Hatshepsut's 22-year reign was one of the most productive construction periods in ancient Egyptian history. She ordered construction of her beautiful mortuary temple beneath the cliffs at Deir el Bahari, enlarged the Karnak Precinct of Mut, and restored ancient buildings destroyed by the Hyksos.

Herodotus: A Greek historian of the fifth century BC, Herodotus visited ancient Egypt around 450 BC during a period of Persian rule. His writings were the first to describe Egyptian religious rituals, festivals, magical rites, and animal cults. Herodotus also wrote about the Great Pyramid at Giza, Memphis, and the Labyrinth of Amenemhet III.

Hor-Aha: The second pharaoh of the First Dynasty and son of King Narmer, Aha ordered construction of Memphis, the capital of united

Egypt. Memphis was one of the world's most important cities for more than three millennia.

Imhotep: The Chancellor of the King of Upper and Lower Egypt, and a great builder, Imhotep was the architect and construction foreman on the Step Pyramid, built for Djoser at Saqqara.

Khufu: As the second pharaoh of the Fourth Dynasty, Khufu ordered the construction of the Great Pyramid of Giza around 2560 BC. The giant structure was to serve as Khufu's tomb, but his mummified remains have never been found.

Narmer: Later called Menes or Meni, "the founder," Narmer united Upper and Lower Egypt through a combination of political will and military conquest, initiating the First Dynasty around 3150 BC.

Ramses II: Also known as Ramses the Great, the pharaoh ruled for 67 years when ancient Egypt was at a pinnacle of power and wealth. Ramses II conquered Syria, Libya, and Nubia and ordered major construction projects including the Colossus of Ramses. He had 200 wives and concubines, 96 sons and 60 daughters, and lived to be 96 years old.

Tutankhamen: Known as King Tut, Tutankhamen is the most famous of the Egyptian pharaohs because of the treasures discovered intact in his tomb in AD 1922. When Tut came to power at the age of nine, around 1334 BC, Egypt was in turmoil because of religious battles. During his short, nine-year reign, Tut and his advisers helped restore order to the kingdom.

For Further Research

Books

Pamela Dell, *Hatshepsut: Egypt's First Female Pharaoh*. Mankato, MN: Compass Point, 2008.

Joann Fletcher, *Exploring the Life, Myth, and Art of Ancient Egypt*. New York: Rosen, 2009.

Belinda Gallagher, ed., *100 Things You Should Know About Pyramids*. Essex, UK: Miles Kelly, 2009.

Charles George, *Pyramids*. San Diego: ReferencePoint, 2007.

Norman Bancroft Hunt, *Living in Ancient Egypt*. New York: Chelsea House, 2008.

Kathleen Kuiper, ed., *Ancient Egypt: From Prehistory to the Islamic Conquest*. New York: Rosen, 2010.

Virginia Schomp, *The Ancient Egyptians*. New York: Benchmark, 2007.

Silvia Anne Sheafer, *Ramses the Great*. New York: Chelsea House, 2008.

Adam Woog, *Mummies*. San Diego: ReferencePoint, 2008.

Websites

Egypt: Land of Eternity (http://ib205.tripod.com/book.html). An extremely detailed site published by British Egyptologist Ian Bolton, featuring assorted information about ancient kings and queens, gods and goddesses, mythology, tombs, and monuments.

Gateway to Ancient Egypt (www.gatewaytoancientegypt.co.uk). Through pictures, text, and maps, this site explores the lives of ancient

Egyptian rulers, significant historical events, religious beliefs, and the monuments still standing today.

Giza Archives (www.gizapyramids.org). This site, hosted by the Museum of Fine Art (MFA) Boston, contains tens of thousands of photographs, maps, digitized articles, and records of tomb, monument, and object excavations. They are compiled from the single longest-running Giza excavation, conducted by Harvard University and the MFA between 1902 and 1947. The site also features interactive Web technologies, such satellite photos and over 1,000 panoramic views of the site on Quicktime Virtual Reality.

Nova **Online: Pyramids** (www.pbs.org/wgbh/nova/pyramid). This site allows visitors to wander through the chambers and passageways of the Great Pyramids and learn about the pharaohs who built them. Interviews, maps, illustrations, and photographs bring the pyramids to life and provide a unique understanding of the royal tombs.

Pharaonic Egypt (www.reshafim.org.il/ad/egypt/index.html). A comprehensive site with hundreds of pages dedicated to ancient Egyptian history, dynasties, mythology, society, and culture. Detailed interpretations of ancient letters, hieroglyphic inscriptions, and papyrus texts are provided.

Pyramid Texts **Online** (www.pyramidtextsonline.com). This site features the complete English translation and the complete hieroglyphic version of the *Pyramid Texts* along with satellite maps and numerous photos of the pyramid complex at Saqqara.

Tour Egypt (www.touregypt.net/ancientegypt). This website, hosted by Egypt's Ministry of Tourism, contains 5,000 pages of information about ancient Egypt. Essays about nearly every dynasty and pharaoh are available along with excerpts from temple inscriptions and famous writings including the *Pyramid Texts*, the *Coffin Texts*, and the *Book of the Dead*.

Travellers in Egypt (www.travellersinegypt.org). Articles and journals by historical travelers to Egypt and Near East. The writings cover many centuries, from Herodotus to nineteenth-century Egyptologists and twentieth-century American tourists.

Index

Note: Boldface page numbers indicate illustrations.

Abu Simbel temples, 68
afterlife
    food for, 23, 31
    funerary goods for, 18
    immortality for all, 46, 52–53
    of pharaohs, 28, 30
    See also death beliefs
agriculture, **19**
    beginning of, 13
    climate and, 13
    with hunting-gathering, 16
    Nile River and, 13–14
    projects adding land for, 48
    taxes and, 24
Aha (pharaoh), 22, 24
Ahmose I or Amosis I (pharaoh), 58, 59
Aket (inundation season), 13
Akhenaten (Effective Spirit of Aten,
    pharaoh), 66, 86
Aldred, Cyril, 20
Alexander the Great, 69, 72, 86
Alexander VI (pope), 74
Amenemhet I (pharaoh), 6
    assassination of, 47
    construction by, 44–45
    justification of rule, 44, 46–47
    military victories, 45
    as ruler of nome, 41–42
Amenemhet III (pharaoh), 43, 48–50
Amenemhet IV (pharaoh), 53
Amenemhet-Itj-Tawy ("Amenemhet,
    Seizer of the Two Lands"), 44
Amenhotep IV (pharaoh), 66, 86
Ameny (divine savior), 46
Amun or Amun-Re (god of creation)
    and Hatshepsut, 64
    restoration as supreme deity, 67
    temple at Karnak for, 57, 60–61, 67

ancient Egypt
    influence of, 10
    map, 12
ancient Greece
    cultural influence of, 69
    Egyptian religion and, 72
    as transmitters of Egyptian culture, 70,
        80
ancient Romans, 81
Apepi (pharaoh), 55–57
Apis, 74
Appartamenti Borgia, 74
archeology and climate, 16
architecture, 79–81
    See also Karnak Temple complex;
        pyramids
artifacts, 74, 76–77
arts, 14, 49–50
Ascending Passage (of Great Pyramid), 36
astrology, 73
Aten (god), 66

ba (life force), 27–28
barks (boats), 30
barrages, 48
Battle of Avaris, 58
Bauval, Robert, 36, 38
Bedouin nomads, 44
beer, 31
Bent Pyramid, 32
Betto, Bernadino di, 74
black land, 11
Black Pyramid at Dahshur, 48–59, **49**
Book of Gates, 63
Book of the Dead, 19–20, **19**, 63, **65**
burials
    of American founding fathers, 80
    food for afterlife, 23, 31
    funerary goods, 18
    mastaba tombs, 23
    See also pyramids

Burstein, Stanley, 70
Burton, Richard, 70

calendar, 13
Carter, Howard, 67
Champollion, Jean-François, 9–10, 77
chariots, 60
"Chiefs of Foreign Lands." *See* Hyksos
Christianity, 73
City of the Falcon (Hierakonpolis, White
    Land), 14
civil war, 40
climate, 13, 16
Coffin Texts, 51–53
Colossus of Ramses, 68, 87
columns, 79–80

Dahshur, 32
death beliefs
    food for afterlife, 23, 31
    funerary goods for afterlife, 18
    immortality for all, 46, 52–53
    immortality of pharaohs, 23, 25, 27
    ka, 25, 27
    mummification, 27–28, 29
    pharaohs' ascension to heaven, 28, 30
    weighing of heart, 19–20
    See also Osiris
deities, 18–20, **19**
delta, Nile River
    in ancient times, 15–16
    flooding, 13
    location, 11
Descending Passage (of Great Pyramid),
    34–35, 36
Description de l'Égypte, 76
Deshret region, 11
diet, 31
Diodorus of Sicily, 73
Djoser (pharaoh), 30, 86
Doric columns, 80
drought season, 13
Duat, 52–53
Dynasty Zero (Naqada Dynasty), 6,
    14–15

Ebers Medical Papyrus, 79, 81
Edelson, Stuart M., 68
Edwin Smith Papyrus, 51, 77
Egyptian revival, 74

Eighteenth Dynasty
    empire, 66, 68
    founded, 7, 58
    internal turmoil, 67
Eleventh Dynasty, 41, 46
*Emerald Tablet of Hermes Trismegistus,
    The,* 72–73
Eye of Providence, 72
Eye of Ra or Eye of Horus, 72

Faiyum Oasis, 48
farming. *See* agriculture
feluccas, **15**
fertility, god of, 18
Fifteenth Dynasty, 56
Fifth Dynasty, 28, 39
First Dynasty, 17, 20, 23–24
    See also Hor-Aha

First Intermediate Period, 40, 42
food, 23, 31
Fourteenth Dynasty, 54
Fourth Dynasty, 39
    See also Khufu

funerary goods, 18, 46

geometry, 71
Gilbert, Adrian, 36, 38
Giza, pyramids at, 25, **26**
    See also Great Pyramid (of King Khufu)
    at Giza
Gleaming Pyramid of the South, 32
Golden Age of the Middle Kingdom, 53
government
    capital, 22
    papyrus and, 17
    religion and, 21
    taxes, 23–24
Grand Gallery (of Great Pyramid), **35,**
    36
Granite Coffer, 38
"Great Hymn to Aten" (Akhenaten), 66
Great Pyramid (of King Khufu) at Giza
    construction of, 25, 33, 34, 37
    interior of, 34–38, **35,** 39
    size of, 33
    U.S. dollar bill and, 72
Great Seal of the United States, 72
Great Sphinx, 38

See also Great Pyramid (of King Khufu) at Giza
Green, Frederick, 20–21
Grimal, Nicolas, 51
growing season, 13

Hapi, Hep, or Hepi (god of Nile), 18
Harwerre or Horwerra, 50–51
Hatshepsut (queen), 63–64, 86
  tomb of, 62

Hellenistic culture, 70–72
Hermes (god), 72–73
Hermes Trismegistus, 73, 74
Herodotus, 86
  on construction of Great Pyramid at Giza, 33, 34
  on Labyrinth, 43
  on Nile River, 11
Hierakonpolis (White Land), 14
hieroglyphs
  deciphered, 9–10, 77
  development of, 22
  Naqada II culture and, 14
  uses of, 8–9
History of Egypt (Manetho), 56–57
Hor-Aha (pharaoh), 22, 24, 86
Horus (patron god)
  of Hierakonpolis, 14
  of living pharaohs, 18, 19
Hyksos
  Amun-Re and, 60, 61
  conquest by, 54
  expulsion of, 58
  rule of, 55–58
  warfare and, 54
Hypostyle Hall at Karnak, 68

Iamblichus, 71
Imhotep, 30–32, 87
Inene, 60, 61, 64
Institute of Egypt, 76
"Instruction of King Amenemhet," 47
inundation season, 13, 16
Ipuwer, 40
irrigation system, 13–14
Isis, 74

jewelry, 49–50

ka (life force), 25, 27
Kamose (Theban ruler), 57–58
Karnak Temple complex
  building by Ramses II, 68
  building by Tutankhamen, 67
  exploits of Kamose, 57
  exploits of Thutmose III, 64–65
  obelisks at, 80
  Precinct of Amun at, 60–61
Kemet, 11
Khafre (pharaoh), 38
Khety, 47
Khufu (pharaoh), 6, 25, 33, 87
  See also Great Pyramid (of King Khufu) at Giza
King's Chamber (of Great Pyramid), 36–38
King Tut. *See* Tutankhamen
Kush, 53–54, 58

Labyrinth, 43
Land of the Papyrus Plant, 16
Late Period, 69
Lauer, Jean-Philippe, 31–32
legacy of ancient Egypt
  architecture, 79–81
  mathematics, 70–71
  medicine, 77, 79, 81
  record keeping, 8–9
  transfer to West of, 70–72, 74
Leo X (pope), 74
Lincoln Memorial, 80
literature, 51–53
Louvre Pyramid, 81
Lower Egypt (Red Lands)
  life in, 16–17, 20
  Naqada Dynasty and, 14
  reunification with Upper Egypt, 42
  See also delta

Manetho, 56–57
mastaba tombs, 23
mathematics, 70–71
medicine, 77, 79, 81
Meidum, pyramids at, 32
Memphis, as capital, 22
Menes or Meni (pharaoh), 20
Menkaure (pharaoh), 38–39
Merimden beni Salame (Lower Egypt), 16
Merimden culture, 16

Mertz, Barbara, 16
Middle Kingdom, 42–43
  See also Amenemhet I
Mills, Robert, 80
monotheism, 66
mortuary temples, 34, 43
mummification, 27–28, **29, 56**
museum exhibits, 8

Napoléon Bonaparte, 74, 75, 76
Naqada Dynasty (Dynasty Zero), 14–15
Naqada II culture, 14–15
Narmer (pharaoh), 20–21, 87
Narmer palette, 21
Nekhen (White Land), 14
New Kingdom
  conquests, 55, 65
  end of, 69
  foundations for, 58
  as military state, 58–60
Nile River
  canals and dikes, 13–14
  course, 11
  delta, 11, 13, 15–16
  drought and, 68–69
  feluccas on, 15
  god of, 18
  importance of, 11
  inundation and taxes, 24
  Senusret III irrigation project, 48
nilometer, 24
Nineteenth Dynasty, 68
nomes (settlements), 16, 41–42
Nubia, 59

obelisks, 80
Old Kingdom, 25, 40
Osiris (god of the underworld), 19, 45
  about, 19
  immortality for all, 46, 52–53
  at Vatican, 74
  weighing of heart of the dead, 19–20

pantheism, 66
papyrus, 16, 17
peasants, 31, 32–33
Pei, I.M., 81
Peret (growing season), 13
pharaohs
  afterlife, 28, 30

  age of, 21
  first of united Egypt, 20, 21
  as immortal god-king, 23, 25, 27
  patron god of living, 18
  successors to Hor-Aha, 24
population, 21
Prisse d'Avennes, Achille Constant
  Théodore Émile, 51
Prisse Papyrus, 51, 52
"Prophesy of Neferti," 46–47
Ptolemy V (king of Egypt), 76
pyramids
  of Amenemhet I, 44
  of Amenemhet III, 48–49, 49
  beliefs about, 10
  Bent at Dahshur, 32
  conditions needed for, 25
  construction of, 32–33
  decline in workmanship of, 39–40
  at Giza, 25, 26
  in Labyrinth, 43
  at Meidum, 32
  modern, 81
  Roman, 81
  at Saqqara, 28, 30, 39
  as stairways to heaven, 30
  tourists, 25
  on U.S. dollar bill, 72
  Valley of the Kings, 12, 61, 62
  See also Great Pyramid (of King Khufu)
    at Giza
Pyramid Texts, 28, 51
Pythagoras, 71

Queen's Chamber (of Great Pyramid), 36
Quibell, James, 20–21

Ra-Harakhte (god), 66
Ramses II, the Great (pharaoh), **56, 62,**
  68, 87
Ra or Re (sun god), 18
record keeping, 8–9
red land, 11
Red Lands. *See* Lower Egypt (Red Lands)
religion
  adoption by other cultures, 71–73
  Akhenaten and, 66
  conversion to Christianity, 73
  government and, 21
  overview of, 18

Tutankhamen and, 67
See also death beliefs; specific gods
Renaissance, 74
Rosetta Stone, 76–77, 78

Saqqara, pyramids at, 28, 30, 39
scribes, 22–24
seasons, 13
Second Intermediate Period, 53–54
Senusret, Senuwosret, or Sesostris
(pharaoh), 47–48
Senusret II (pharaoh), 48
Shemu (drought season), 13
ships, 15, 59, 65
Sixth Dynasty, 39, 40
Sneferu (pharaoh), 32, 46
Sobekneferu (queen), 53
Step Pyramid, 30–32
Subterranean Chamber (of Great
Pyramid), 35–36

Taa II (Theban ruler), 57
Tale of the Shipwrecked Sailor, The, 51
taxes
beer as payment, 31
during First Dynasty, 23–24
during Intermediate Period, 42
Terraces of Turquoise, 50
Theban people, 56–58
theocracy, 21
Third Intermediate Period, 69
Thirteenth Dynasty, 53–54
Thoth (god), 72
Thutmose I (pharaoh), 59–61, 62, 63
Thutmose II (pharaoh), 62, 63–64
Thutmose III (pharaoh), 62, 64–65
trade, 17
turquoise mines, 50

Tutankhamen (King Tut, pharaoh),
87
ascension to throne, 8, 66–67
death, 8, 9
museum exhibit about, 8
religion and, 67
tomb of, 62, 63, 67
Tutankhamen and the Golden Age of
Pharaohs (museum exhibit), 8
Twelfth Dynasty
end of, 53
founded, 40, 42
irrigation of Nile and prosperity, 48
jewelry, 49–50
literature, 51–53
Twentieth Dynasty, 68–69

underworld, god of, 19–20, 19
United States, Great Seal of, 72
Upper Egypt (White Land)
importance of, 15
life in, 14, 20
location and geography, 14
reunification with Lower Egypt, 42

Valley of the Kings, 61, 62, 63
Valley of the Queens, 63
Vatican, 74
volcanic eruption, 41

Walls of the Ruler, 44
warfare and Hyksos, 54
Washington, DC, 80
Washington Monument, 80
White Land. See Upper Egypt (White
Land)
Wild Bull, The (ship), 59
writing. See hieroglyphs, papyrus

Picture Credits

About the Author

Stuart A. Kallen is the author of more than 250 nonfiction books for children and young adults. He has written on topics ranging from the theory of relativity to the history of rock and roll. In addition, Kallen has written award-winning children's videos and television scripts.